Catherine Hytner was born the unwant
Handsome Yorkshire plumber and a *Terminally Vain* arty half Irish mother
in a 1950's working-class, inner city suburb of Manchester. Her neglected
childhood years were spent always finding somewhere else to be, often
at a hidden cost.

The 1960's see Cathy wholeheartedly embracing the cultural revolution
to the full, but not making it to London.

In the 1970's after a brief unsuccessful attempt to build security on a
shaky foundation, she comes out of it with a daughter to fend for too. She
now enters a world where she is exploited in the media, like so many
others at this time. Even when she gets a regular gig, that on the surface
would appear to be a success, she suffers at the hands of the men who
wield the power,

Until, she finally says..." No more of this" and seeks a more cerebral and
respected path...

These are Catherine's memories.

COUNTDOWN CATH

Memories of
Cathy Hytner

APS Books
Stourbridge

APS Books
4 Oakleigh Road,
Stourbridge,
West Midlands,
DY8 2JX

APS Books is a subsidiary of the APS Publications imprint

www.andrewsparke.com

First published worldwide by APS Books in 2020

ISBN 978-1-78996-201-7

1

FANNY LILLIAN

Fanny Lillian McCarthy (nee Downey) was my grandma. She lived in a prefab on Princess road, which is now the M56 into Manchester from the south. My grandfather had died in the bedroom there and so I avoided that part of the house which meant never going to use the bathroom. I have only one recollection of him visiting as a five-year-old one summer with my elder sister. He had been reclining in a deck chair by the garden shed, wearing suit trousers, a white collarless shirt, braces and a hat. We had been given salad, which in 1955 consisted of lettuce with slices of egg, cucumber, tomato, and beetroot served on this occasion with a tin of salmon between us. All of which I hated. Grandad coaxed me that if I ate it all up "like a good little girl" then I would get a sweet. I took this to mean a sweetie sweet but it turned out to be a dessert of tinned peaches and condensed milk which I hated even more. I bore a grudge.

Granny had a predisposition to melancholy and a budgie called *Lickle Mickey Macky*. The only thing he ever said was "Lickle Mickey Macky, he's a bew beauty" in a fine imitation of grandma's voice. His cage was never closed and he sat happily by choice on his own doorstep.

Fanny Lillian never ever visited our house. It seems that early on in the days after the marriage of Jack and Dot, she had visited on a Thursday afternoon at a set time. One fateful afternoon she had arrived early and seated at the kitchen table had witnessed Jack's impersonation of her. He had affected a bow-legged, swaying walk stooped close to the ground whilst cackling in a falsetto voice.

To Jack's delight and Dot's chagrin she had waddled out vowing never to return. She kept her word and didn't.

Timothy McCarthy was a lapsed catholic from Dublin, Fanny Lillian Downey a seamstress from Hulme. They had been a devoted couple. Timothy was a diabetic and despite Fanny Lillian's meticulous weighing and monitoring of his food intake, he died shortly after retirement.

Granny's next door neighbour had "a bag" on her side which was always talked about in the same exaggerated mimed whisper usually reserved for talking about *women's problems*. I was both fascinated and horrified by this and could never concentrate on anything she said as I was busy imagining where it was, what it looked like and whether or not it required emptying.

Every Thursday I visited Granny straight from school. Sometimes I was on the school Special Number 22 bus, at other times on my bike.

The routine was to cut the grass front and back, clip both hedges, have a meal which was either home-boiled ham, home-boiled beetroot and crinkle cut chips, or creamed mushrooms on toast. Granny still baked once a week making scones to use up sour milk but that was on a Friday unfortunately. I used to cut her hair for her in a kind of 1920's flapper style at the front and huge chunky steps at the back.

Then the Meski's ice cream van would come round, even in winter, and we would have a wafer each whilst Fanny Lillian trounced me at Gin Rummy.

I knew all of Granny's stories by heart. She was one of thirteen children, several of whom "had been taken in the night by croup" She had had pneumonia as a child and the doctor had called round just before mealtime to drain off fluid in a crude and excruciating manner and "You know what? I completely lost my appetite." She had managed to fall into the dolly tub one wash day and still bore the scars.

She used to say that people waited until she ventured out if it were perhaps only to collect her pension or to " get in a bit o' shoppin'," so that they could slip a note through the front door to say they had called and "What a shame" she had been out. I thought this might very well have been the case.

When Timothy McCarthy's retirement clock chimed seven-forty-five I could sign off from my granny's.

I was in fact cycling home from Withington to Levenshulme when the news of President Kennedy's assassination broke.

2

PICTURE THIS JANUARY 1950

The photograph is in black and white. There are two rows of shops facing each other at the bottom of a hill, just before crossroads. The road signs read Slade Lane, Albert Road, and Mosley Road. These Victorian shops are uniform in appearance. They have plate glass windows surrounded by mahogany wood surrounds beneath signs displaying the names of each family run businesses. From left to right on the south side is W. Sykes (Grocer), J.M. Mawson (Plumber), J.W. Mills (Newsagent), and S. Davies (Baker), next to which is a triangle of grassy wasteland known locally as *the dog's toilet*. The year is 1950 and dogs were customarily let out to wander the streets and do as they pleased. On the north side is A Monks (Sweets), N Williams (Insurance Broker), Marion Davies (Costumier) Cretney's (Cobbler) and Albert Saunders (Green grocer).

Around the window of J.M. Mawson is gathered a small crowd. There are women in their floral wrap-around pinafores with their hair scooped up into no-nonsense headscarves tied at the front in a double bow. One is still holding her metal bucket and donkey stone. Another has her sleeves rolled up and flour on her forearms. One balances a snotty baby on an out-slung hip. Two of the local shopkeepers stand behind them in their utilitarian brown overalls. One has the big black built up shoe of the crippled cobbler, Mr. Cretney, the other a trade mark dog-end hanging from the corner of his mouth often catching the permanent dew drop escaping from his nose. He is Albert Saunders, the Green grocer.

There is a travelling salesman distinguishing himself from the others by a suit and a trilby hat, his well-worn case of wares held in his leather gloved right hand. Two men in overalls and flat caps stand beside him with their Woodbines held inside cupped hands perhaps to avoid sniper's bullets from the long-ago trenches of world war one. Standing out from the crowd is a pretty, teenaged girl who has the high swishy ponytail of a show pony. Her tiny waist is encompassed in a deep elasticated waspy belt from which sticks out a circular skirt held proud by stiff underskirts starched in sugar and water. There is a neckerchief tied jauntily to the left of her throat and on her feet are flat ballerina pumps of red leather. She lives next door at Sykes's and will become an *It girl* called Sabrina in the near future.

What begins as a titter soon grows into a howl of laughter as those in front point and put cupped hands to spluttering mouths. Those at the back strain tip toed to see through the gaps. More and more passers-by join the throng.

It is a black, cold, drizzly January night against which the illuminated shop window stands out. It is dressed in the style of a highly desirable bathroom comprising a close-coupled symphonic W.C, a pedestal washbasin and a bath all arranged upon a mock tiled floor. There is a pile of discarded children's clothes on this floor and a naked toddler is having a pretend bath in her solitary imagined game of house.

Suddenly the good-natured atmosphere evaporates as from the back of the crowd a tall muscular man in overalls carrying a tool bag pushes through the crowd shouldering them out of the way. He pushes open the shop door setting off the jolly jingle of the brass bell above. Before the sound has finished vibrating through the air his cry is heard. "What the bloody hell?"

It sends the toddler scampering out of sight and revealed on the shop floor in front of him is a heavily pregnant woman on all fours mid-contraction screaming.

"Jack, Jack. Thank god! It's time to go."

3

80 ALBERT ROAD

Number 80 Albert Road was a Victorian house where the Rackham family had lived for three generations. The front door opened onto a long dark hallway with the obligatory hall stand by the door into the main reception room off to the left. This formal room was set out to receive visitors. Visitors who no longer called. The three-piece suite with its antimacassars along the back rests was set out on a plush-patterned carpet. There was a piano against the wall, a display cabinet full of china and silverware, a fireplace with a brass coal scuttle and an iron hearth set placed upon its lovely green tiles. The bay window was dressed with elaborate lace nets and faded green velvet curtains. In the bay stood a table upon which there was a neglected and dusty Aspidistra.

There was a dining room next on the left the door to which was by the bottom of the steep stairs up to the first floor. It too is no longer used. The doorway to the cellar was under the stairs on the right-hand side next to the door into the back room where the big black range was the heart of the house. Off this back room was a tiny scullery. It had a tiny window overlooking the dank sunless back garden, under which there was a Belfast sink. There were wooden shelves holding pots and pans and on the wall over the door was the mahogany glass box containing brass bells that rang according to which cord had been pulled in which room to summon service. Left-over food was put down on the side of the cellar steps the better to keep in the cold and dark.

Up the stairs there was one of the earliest Victorian bathrooms with its original fittings. The wash down porcelain toilet was decorated with blue flowers and served by a cistern high above on the wall from which hung the brass chain. The bath was alongside, cast iron, scroll topped and deep, its huge brass taps never turned on as it stood there unused.

There was a bedroom that looked over the back garden, another which overlooked the side of the house and then the master double bedroom with its two sash windows overlooking the front garden. There was an even steeper, darker staircase that ran from the landing uncarpeted up to the two tiny bedrooms under the eaves.

There was a plot of land adjacent to the house that the Rackham family had rented since day one. It had been the grazing for their pony and it came with its now derelict stable and outbuilding that had housed *the trap*.

Another steep, dark set of steps led to the substantial back kitchen door by the bottom of which stood the shed housing the dolly tub, mangle and stone laundry sink. In its heyday, the bustling house must have been a hive of activity, full with *Pappy, Mamma,* an elderly aunt, two uncles and three children, all served by a cook, liveryman and maid.

By the late 1950's all that remained of this dynasty was a brother and sister, William and Victorine Rackham, who sat day after day either side of the black kitchen range in the back of the house.

The land rented by the Rackhams abutted the end of our garden in Osbourne road. When around eight years old, bored of playing alone with my dolls on the tumbling down Anderson shelter, I had explored a gap in the hedge, wandered across the field and found Bill and Vicky Rackham sitting in deckchairs enjoying strawberries and ice cream in the sunshine - the sun only ever shone down the side of this permanently sombre house. I had been offered some and given my own deckchair. From then on I visited regularly basking in the attention they gave to me.

There were other visitors of course. The vicar called once a week for them to take communion. The coalman shot coal through a hatch on the side of the house directly into the coal hole. Marion Wilson (Costumier) of Slade Lane would call to measure up Miss Rackham and make her bespoke garments. The milkman would leave their daily pint in the porch. Mrs. Heyes, their next-door neighbour would be kept on the doorstep as Victorine thought her common.

They believed in God and Winston Churchill and every morning at eleven o clock Bill Rackham would take a woodbine from his tin and smoke it on Doctor's advice "to loosen the chest"

He had been a precision engineer at Reynolds chains in Crossley Road until forced into early retirement due to a stroke. The left side of his face had dropped. I would avert my eyes when he ate insufficiently cooked egg and bacon, the sight of the snotty slimy egg escaping the corner of his mouth disgusting me.

Victorine had been one of those ladies who had remained single due to the lack of young men coming home from World War One. She had worked all her life at J.W Mills on Slade Lane. Even at my tender age I had concluded from pictures in their album, the way she spoke of him, and some gossip often referred to but never detailed, laid at the feet of Mrs. Heyes, that her relationship with Mr. Mills had been more than that of mere employee.

Bill had been married to Maude, who had died young in the master bedroom. In the album there were sepia pictures of their mother and father, she with curls piled up on top of her head, wearing a striped fitted dress nipped in at the impossible twenty-two inch waist and pulled out into a bustle at the back, he with mutton chop whiskers, and a gold watch chain looped across his front between his waistcoat pockets. The two brothers of *Pappy* looked similar to him, but more rakish. Bill and Vicky told me stories of how they had lost much family money gambling on cock fights. *Pappy* it seemed had had vices too. A story they often told was of when in a drunken rage he had thrown the family silver on the back of the fire. Mother had watched keeping a "poker straight back."

It never occurred to me to ask if she had retrieved it later, but thinking about it now I guess that the maid would have done that. *Mamma* had been an aristocrat who had married unwisely. The photograph album had their Coat of Arms on its leather cover.

They, like my grandmother, repeated their repertoire of stories until I knew them all by heart. They too had made up the dialogue of their lives by linked up stories. They had walked routinely from Levenshulme to Manchester in the winter to skate on the lake in front of the Hospital in Piccadilly Gardens. They would walk regularly to Barcicroft Fields in Heaton Moor to play. They had known "The two Miss Mosley's" who had lived on Burnage Lane and had had a model railway in their grounds. And the Duchess of York hospital had housed some of the broken young men on their return from the trenches.

They told me in great detail who had died in which room in the house, and how. I had already seen pictures of them all in the family album. I felt as though the house were a time warp full of ghosts, and still set out as it had been when they had been flesh moving around in this very space. I once misguidedly agreed to spend the night on a bed put up for me in the dining room, an experience never repeated. I had lain awake for hours wanting to wee but lacking the courage to go upstairs to the bathroom. When I finally did, I negotiated my way sliding my back against the walls, heart pounding.

Vicky and Bill used chamber pots kept under their beds which Bill would empty in the mornings. His shuffling walk and his shaky hand caused choppy waters within the po and occasional waves to break over its sides. For their daily hand and face wash they poured cold water and vinegar from china flower patterned jugs and bowls which sat on their marble topped dressers.

Having their complete attention, I would rattle off my party piece on the piano in the front room leaving the doors open and they would always clap and shout "Bravo" at the end of my stumbling, imperfect rendition. Looking back, in their place I would have found it difficult to keep a straight face, but the Rackhams were serious and dignified people who kept their emotions reined in tight.

Other times I would select a passage from the Bible and a hymn from their book and stand behind the pulled-out table to conduct the service,

We would play a game where one took letters of the alphabet chosen by turns, and had to write down as many names of fruit or vegetables as one could beginning with that letter. We dutifully marked off each other's papers and scored them even though they were mainly the same.

I would make pancakes on the tiny gas ring in the corner of the scullery, which varied wildly in their consistency but were always enthusiastically received.

November 5th would see Bill and myself trying to coax a damp bonfire to light, trying to eat partially cooked, fire-baked potatoes and waving sparklers around writing our names in the air.

Summer would see Bill and myself mowing the grass in their field. I would pull the machine in a makeshift rope yoke and Bill would push and steer from behind.

Late summer would see the three of us sitting in a row by the side of the house, savouring the tiny sweet strawberries just picked from the garden served up with a rectangle of *Wall's ice cream* cut from the block I had just run to Monk's Sweet Shop to buy.

In the shed I would turn the handle on the mangle whilst Bill fed through the big pink bloomers and his grey threadbare long johns with their button up back section. They were as clean as Bill could manage to get them using the block of carbolic and a washing paddle and then lye soap and a washboard for the more stubborn stains.

In spring Bill and I would man-handle the carpet from the back room into the back garden, hang it on the line and attack it with lattice wooden beaters.

I would cut their hair and shave Bill with an open razor. For Vicky Rackham's sparse white hair, I would wind it onto tiny steel curlers in a circle around her hairline.

All this must have come as much needed relief from the monotony of usual days, making shopping lists of things like *two lean lamb chops, half a pound of carrots* or *a packet of suet* which would take Bill half the day to collect in the shopping basket from Brimlows the Butcher, Saunders the Green grocer or Seymore Meads.

I would write down their reminiscences of growing up in Burnage, even though in actual fact they lived in Levenshulme, the border being on Slade Lane by the hospital and Albert Road being clearly on the wrong side of that boundary. They were snobs.

They encouraged me to write poems. "The door creaked, the owl screeched, the vase fell to the floor..." began one of them. "Oh, how I wish that I could be a rider in the show, my horse would be so proud of me, and I would love him so..." was another.

Bill would send these off to the Manchester Evening News and they would be published.

The poem about the horse was a shameless hint to suggest to them that they could buy me a horse. It could graze in the field, live in the shed, I don't know! I hadn't worked out the finer details. For a good few Christmases and Birthdays, I had harboured the hope that they would come good, finally realising that this was never going to happen when I unwrapped the woefully disappointing present of a block of Cadbury's Dairy Milk and two old ping pong bats wrapped in newspaper tied up with string.

By the time I was ten years old, we had moved to Burnage Hall Road and I cut down my visits to just a Saturday afternoon, after my piano lesson with Mrs. Parker back in Osbourne Road.

Early evening Bill would pull out the tiny Black and White television from under the wall cupboard where it was kept on a tea trolley and we would watch *Juke Box Jury* and then *Dixon of Dock Green*. The minute that Constable Dixon had delivered his morality tale from underneath the street- lamp it was time for me to go.

Bill died at the age of sixty-two whilst they were on holiday in Bury St Edmunds and Miss Rackham had another tale to add to her repertoire.

"Bill couldn't eat his meal. He pushed his plate away. I asked him did he want something else. What do you want Bill?" He said, "You know what Vicky, I don't know what I want," and died. This vivid image I stored along with the other stories of the passing of family members family and his ghost was added to the ensemble.

I called as often as I could for a short while trying to help Victorine Rackham by putting talc on her sausage like legs and trying to get her nylons on. I fetched shopping for her and helped her up and down the stairs which was at least some relief from being was forced to accept the triumphant ministrations of Mrs. Heyes who she had previously never allowed over the threshold.

Miss Rackham was soon moved into an old people's home in Longsight and didn't last much longer. This I viewed with relief as I had visited the home only once and found the smell and the old people too much for a twelve-year old. She left a diamond ring for me in her will, but it was never to be found.

4

PICTURE THIS FEBRUARY 1950

It is a bright blue day. The snow drops are peeping up through the grass under the mature spreading lime tree beside the pea gravel drive leading up to the majestic steps and double arched door.

Outside on the wide tree lined cul-de-sac that is Grange Avenue a Volkswagen campervan pulls up and in a fluid spring Jack alights and presses the brass button recessed into one of the pillars either side of the ornamental wrought iron gates. There is something of the Clarke Gable about him, muscular shoulders and upper arms, an inverted triangular shape, thick wavy hair and a pencil thin moustache across the full upper lip. The gates swing open. The Volkswagen workhorse is parked on the driveway. Jack takes a final drag of his cigarette, exhales extravagantly before flicking it from between his thumb and index finger on to the manicured lawn. He bounds up to the front door and treads the ground like an impatient stallion.

After a while the door is opened by a maid in uniform who then stands to one side to allow passage of the lady of the house into the open doorway. Mrs. Marjorie Armstrong, widow of Alderman George Armstrong, takes full advantage of the higher ground afforded her by the top step and looks down at the plumber. She is wearing a box-jacketed, four-pleated tweed skirt suit, sensible laced up leather shoes and lisle stockings covering her heavy lower legs. Her grey-streaked hair is curly and brushed back from her face. Her only concession to adornment is a two-string pearl necklace and two marble sized pearl earrings. The excited smile melts from her face as she sees that Jack is empty handed. He carries nothing at all.

"Jack, where is the baby?"

"Dot put her foot down."

"What do you mean, put her foot down? I've got your money here all ready for you. We had an arrangement, Jack."

"I know. What can I do? She got cold feet. I told her 'What do we need another bloody girl for? What do I need another greedy little mouth to feed for? How the bloody hell can this be? What have I done to deserve four sodding girls?"

"Jack, Jack, Jack, go back and tell her the little girl will lack for nothing. Tell her that she is being selfish. Surely she could do with the money?"

"She doesn't care about the money. She doesn't have to bloody earn it. She takes so long to get into the shop that people steal the toilet paper. They send her into the cellar for half a pound of putty and nick a set of chrome mixer fittings while she buggers about down there. Every bill that drops through that letter box is for me, not her. It's nothing to do with her."

"Well Jack, I don't need to tell you that you have disappointed me. I am dreadfully upset. It makes no sense. There you are with your burgeoning brood of little girls you never wanted and here am I with everything to give to this little mite who would be my life now that Alderman Armstrong is gone and I am all alone in this big place. It would all be hers one day."

"Well Mrs. Armstrong, there won't be any more, thank Christ. They've kept her in for a hysterectomy. I've been left with all this lot to cope with on my own. I've cleared a shelf of beans and rice pudding in Sykses. I can't go on like this. I'll have to get my mother in. Not hers, she's bloody 'opless. My mother knows what she's doing. My mother could make a meal out of a scrubbing brush."

"You'll need to excuse me now Jack. I need to go for a lie down. You know how much this meant to me."

"Me too, Mrs. Armstrong, me too !"

"You promised me, Jack. You gave your word. You have let me down "

"I know Mrs. Armstrong. Don't bloody go on. I would do it, but it's her - you know what she's like."

"Jack, just go. See him off the premises Albert"

5

PICTURE THIS 1955

In an attic two sisters, one aged six and one aged nine are lying on a double bed covered with old grey blankets. The walls are bare plaster, the floor wooden boards and the skylight window above their bed has ice around its corners, on the inside.

On the bare plaster there are the words to a song written in crayon. Doris Day. *Once I had a secret love.*

The younger of the two girls stands on a chair and sings the song belting out the chorus dramatically, imagining the chair to be the hill from which she's shouting!

"Now, I shout it from the highest hill; even told the golden daffodil..."

They hear music coming from the attic of the next building across the narrow passageway.

The two girls press their faces against the window to watch the dance class being conducted in the *Muriel Neat School of Dancing*.

The piano thumps and the room is brightly lit against the dark sky. The little ballerinas turn and spin and tap shuffle tap along to *This is Mickey Mouse's birthday party*.

They watch in wonder and admiration until suddenly they are spotted by the teacher and the curtains are drawn closed cutting the scene to black.

It is at this precise moment that the six-year-old vows to herself that when she is grown she will never ever be again on the outside looking in.

6

MONA AND KEN

The age of twelve and a half saw me in the employ of Mona and Ken, at Cowlishawe's Greengrocers. They had moved from Gee Cross in Hyde to Levenshulme. The Hyde and Ashton area was where Myra Hindley and Ian Brady must have been busy meeting around this time.

Mona and Ken had such different accents to us locals. They came from no more than fifteen miles away but spoke a different language.

"Est ew gettena cawd Key 'Ol?" I grew to understand meant "Have you got a cold, Kate?"

She called me *Key'ol* after a cartoon character called *Keyhole Kate*. I didn't mind; it was better than being ignored.

Mona's party piece was to deliver lavish raised leg farts whilst playing an imaginary set of bagpipes tucked under her right arm. She would then grunt with relief and pleasure and exclaim, "Eeeee, she's shot t' cat."

Ken would always pull the same pained face and rebuke her "Oooh Mona!" And then tut and shake his head.

She would pull an exact copy of his facial expression and mimic his voice, "Oooh Ken!" After her riposte she would jauntily carry on with whatever she was doing with a deadpan face.

Mona was budgie-shaped. She had to wear enormous shell-pink, armour-plated brassieres to support her low-slung bosom. When dressed up, her birdlike legs would be encased in American tan nylons which would wrinkle around her delicate ankles. She wore twinsets and tailored, straight woollen skirts which settled demurely on the knee. In summer she wore slippers and in winter brown suede, fur-lined bootees which were ankle length and zipped up the front. She was a martyr to bunions and corns. Both slippers and bootees had been beaten into submission by constant wearing, together with some modification with the scissors. Mona would take a razor blade to her corns resulting in plasters around her toes and she always wore ankle socks to work in.

Ken was thin and ashen with receded brown hair, combed back and often "cut te t' wood." He wore a brown overall in the shop.

I always wore the same jumper and a pair of tartan trews. Fashion was as yet a stranger to me. I would go to the shop on a Friday night straight from school. It was open until quarter to seven. Then we would go upstairs for supper, always the same, always grilled odd shaped ends of fish *what wanted eatin'* topped with bright orange breadcrumbs from a cardboard tube along with a dollop of mashed potatoes and either swede and carrot or spring cabbage. The spring cabbage often contained little black flies about which I learned not to quibble as Mona would always quip "Don't tell anyone, else they'll all want some" or "Added protein, an fer nowt."

After supper Mona would run a steaming hot bath and disappear for her weekly soak whilst Ken and I would go downstairs to make up the orders for tomorrow. We put each order into saved boxes of either cardboard, which had contained Cox's Orange Pippins, Macintosh Reds or Geest bananas, which we checked for stowaway spiders first, or little ply-wood boxes which had held Spanish tomatoes and were more robust. The bill and the address would be dropped into the top of the box. Simple and effective. We never seemed to mix them up - it was a good system, a pencil and a bit of paper. Spanish tomatoes were always cheaper than English *toms* in the same way that *Lincoln* potatoes were cheaper than *Edwards*. We had Hake, Cod and Plaice on the fish slab. On the semi-circular, mirrored, three-tiered display unit which was Mona's pride and joy we normally had Chrysanthemums and dahlias apart from spring when we had daffodils, tulips and irises, "When they werrr reeznable."

How people would have been aghast had they known they were categorised behind their backs by Mona according to the choices they made. People were firstly judged by whether or not they bought flowers at all, and then split depending on whether they bought "Crysants" or Dahlias. The Dahlias often harboured earwigs and cost 1/11d, whereas, Chrysanthemums cost 3/3d, but as Ken always said, "They last much longer you know."

So, if one purchased King Edward potatoes, English tomatoes, Hake and Chrysanthemums, as far as Mona was concerned, you were top notch.

There was an influx of Irish families into Levenshulme at this time. The cheerful, cheeky men worked as labourers and were known for their drunkenness. Their more fraught and harassed wives cleaned for someone or other and were surrounded by babies in bockety prams. There were newborns swaddled in blankets inside, bigger babies seated on top and toddlers clinging to the sides, riding shotgun. Mona would call them "The fifteen pounds of spuds Brigade." No Chrysanthemums for them.

When we had Jersey new potatoes early in the season, Mona would tell everyone that there was a bank loan available with every purchase and confide "Eeee! but they're worth it." However, I don't recall our ever having any potatoes to eat other than mash.

Mona would keep dodgy bruised apples and yellowing leeks - from which she had stripped the outer leaves - under the counter and would work these into the purchases of those not paying close attention. When later Ken would take her on one side to whisper admonishment, she would break free from him and indignantly declare "We've ad te pay fer em Kenbo. Yer too soft you are; yew always were."

When Ken and I had completed the orders, we would line up the boxes along the downstairs passage. This led to *the back* where we had our elevenses on Saturday mornings, in front of the open fire. Elevenses were either Eccles cakes or buttered scones, accompanied by instant coffee made with half water and half evaporated milk. One never lingered too long in *the back* or Mona would shout down the corridor "Ave yew gon te sleep in theeer."

And anyway, if you got too warm by the fire you had a hell of a job re-acclimatising to the Arctic conditions back in the shop, with its ever-open door.

Outside the shop were displayed our more impressive fruits, such as apricots and plums. These had to be fetched in, at the double, if rain were imminent, and then the blinds would be wound down to protect the rest in an exciting race against time.

Ken would hop into Mona's bath water and I would go down to mop the shop floor. All the time Mona would be calling down, "Ey keyol', yew'd best not be at them apricots."

"No," I would splutter, it being hard to say anything more with a mouthful of apricots and almonds.

Ken would emerge from the bathroom, slightly pink but fully clothed again, except for having exchanged his shoes for slippers.

We would watch *The Saint* on television in the lounge, his appearance prompting lewd suggestions from Mona. She fancied Simon Templar something rotten. Ironic really as Ken looked like Roger Moore. She would dole out chocolates to Ken and myself pre-chosen by her from the open box on her knee. Later Ken would let me out of the shop and I would sprint the short distance home.

My mother would come into the shop on a Saturday morning and I would speed up so as to be able to serve her. Mona would always *head me off at the pass* lest I should give my mum good weight.

After the Saturday morning rush, Mona and I would systematically scrub all the surfaces of the shop, ending with a further mopping of the black and white tiled floor. This was then covered with sheets of newspaper until it dried. Mona cursed under her breath anyone showing the insensitivity to come in before the floor was dry.

Mona could jump into the air, raise her right leg to waist height, bring up her left leg, click ankles in mid-air and land again on the spot.

Thirty-five years later I bumped into an elderly woman whom I recognised as having been one of the teachers at the Muriel Neat School of Dancing, back in the day, when in her prime. I asked for news of the Cowlishawes and she looked me straight in the eye, without a shred of sentiment and said "They moved to Blackpool, and Mona had her leg off."

I didn't think to ask which one, whether it was the clicker or the clickee, and concluded that it probably had had more to do with the twenty Players she had smoked every day than the acrobatics.

Mona and Ken paid me twenty- five shillings for my work at the shop. Towards the end of my period of employment there I had worked out a system. I would occasionally ring up 1/11d when the bill had come to £1.1/11d. I would place a postcard in front of the missing first digit that should have popped up in the display markers, corresponding to the keys that had been pressed. The pound note, neatly folded. was slipped down my sock. From the age of thirteen and a half I was never short of money.

On Saturday afternoons after Ken had brushed and mopped out the van. He would don his light blue and white scarf and bobble hat and "Go a watchin' City."

After supper, always dead on six o clock, I would unwrap the scarf and rollers from Mona's hair and tease it into the perfect *Principal Boy* hairstyle, complete with two kiss curls inclining from her temples on to her fore head.

She would soak her fingernails in bleach and hot water to "get the spud muck from under em" and then these perfect, strong talons would be painted deep red. She would then slip into the American tan nylons, a pair of white plastic kitten heels, a pencil skirt and perhaps a sparkly gold or silver lamé top, before completing the look with a cupid-bow mouth of deep red lipstick.

My lasting impression of Mona and Ken on a Saturday evening would be of Mona sitting regally in the front passenger side of the van, smiling benevolently, both hands placed on the clasp of the white plastic handbag placed on her knee, as she was driven by her proud footman, Ken, to Gee Cross Working Men's Club.

7
PICTURE THIS MR. SMITH

It's a mid-summer afternoon. The sun is high in the sky. Cat mint, Marigolds, Nasturtiums and Sweet-peas fight for space in the garden of the family house in Osbourne Road. Dot is playing the piano. Soft lyrical Irish tunes such as *Rose of Tralee* and *Danny Boy* hang in the air. She has sent the little girl next door to collect the rent from Mr. Smith in Bedsit Number Three.

Mr. Smith has thin brown hair brylcreamed and slicked back from his clean-shaven, bespectacled, lean face. He has on a shirt minus its detachable collar with the top button eased for comfort. His braces are dropped from his shoulders and loop around the top of his grey suit trousers. He has on grey and red felt slippers.

He opens his door and looks down at the little girl. She has blonde curls pulled back from a side parting into a shabby red ribbon. She has on a blue and white gingham dress over which is a hand-knitted, bottle-green cardigan. She wears grubby white ankle socks and black pumps.

"Me mum says can she have our rent please." She holds out her hand in a business-like manner pleased to have relayed the message without fault.

"Oh, she did, did she? Well you'd better come in then."

He says as he stands to one side and gestures a sweeping bow with a flourish of his right hand. "Come on in if you please."

There is a lone moquette chair in the centre of the room in front of a green and cream utilitarian kitchen unit. It comprises two rippled glass top cupboards, a hinged work-top that drops down for use above two closed, cream, wooden doors. There is a single bed along the sash window from which hang orange and brown fibre-glass curtains from a metal rail. On the opposite wall there is a sink unit with a drainer and a Baby Belling cooker on a makeshift worktop, below which is a set of shelves closed off with a small curtain of the same material as that over the main window.

The flooring is brown and green patterned linoleum, covered in the centre by a dusty worn carpet upon which stands the Bex Bissel carpet sweeper, abandoned where Mr. Smith had been mid-sweep before answering the knock on the door.

"Just let me get the rent book. Now, where did I put it? No, not in here, let me think...just going to make a spam buttie. Would you like one?" he says with a smile.

"Oh yes please," replies little Cath.

He takes a small brown loaf from the kitchenette top cupboard, places it on the work top on a wooden bread board and sets about meticulously cutting four thin slices. He spreads them thinly with Blue Band margarine, opens the tin of spam with its key, taps out the pale pink oblong from which he then carves two slithers. He makes two sandwiches that he cuts neatly into quarters putting each onto a plate, before handing one to the little girl.

She perches on the arm of the chair as they sit together to eat the sandwiches. "Would you like to meet some of my little friends?" asks Mr. Smith.

"Yes," says Cath.

"Alright then, you just finish off your buttie and I'll draw the curtains."

In the darkened room Mr. Smith angles the bedside lamp to shine onto the wall between the bed-head and the kitchenette. Then he uses his hand to create a tree, then a snake, then a bird, weaving a tale around them. Cath watches spellbound.

"...And then night fell, and they all went to bed" finishes the story as Mr. Smith lowers her onto his knee, takes out his stiff purple dick and places it in her hand.

Meanwhile, Dot has moved on from her Irish Folk song repertoire and is now perfecting her version of *Take Five* the Dave Brubeck hit of the day, remarkable for its complicated 5/4 rhythm. She plays by ear and is lost in the moment.

Jack steps out of the doorway, where he has been standing for a while and causes Dot to stop abruptly and jump up in startled guilt.

"So, this is what you do all day when I'm out workin'. No wonder I've got no clean bloody socks."

"I've only this minute sat down. I've never stopped all day."

"Well, put kettle on, Dot. I'm spittin' feathers 'ere."

They walk along the hallway to the back room where they are sitting drinking tea from blue and white stripped mugs when the little girl comes running in breathless through the kitchen door.

"Ah, there you are," says Dot. "No rent I see. I don't know, if you want a thing doing, do it yourself!"

"Just run to the ciggie machine for us will you Might Mouse, an get us ten players," says Jack. "I'll time you."

Jack gives the little girl a two-shilling piece and he and Dot turn away back to their conversation.

The little girl closes her hand over the coin and sets off down the hallway and out of the front door. She runs to the end of Osbourne Road, darts across the busy main road, puts the two shilling piece into the shiny silver cigarette dispenser outside J.W. Mills Newsagents, pulls open the drawer retrieves the packet of cigarettes, collects the penny change from its dish, re-crosses the main road, runs back along Osbourne road, through the front door of Number 83, along the hallway, and with eager panting pride presents Jack with the results of her efforts. Without turning or halting his conversation, other than to smirk at Dot and count out "Four hundred and eighty seconds."

He takes the packet, opens it, taps a cigarette on the packet and lights up.

8

PICTURE THIS TICK TOCK

It's 1960. In the Victorian kitchen a pre-pubescent girl is carefully mixing eggs into flour and then slowly adding milk to avoid getting lumps. The gas ring is already on heating up the frying pan into which she deftly slips a slither of lard. She pours the mixture into a cup until it is half full. When the lard has melted she swirls the mixture into the pan leaving it just long enough to set before slipping a spatula underneath and flipping the pancake over. When cooked, she places it carefully on a plate and repeats the procedure until there is a neat stack. She takes three plates down from the shelf and places two pancakes on each plate before sprinkling them with sugar, squirting them with lemon and rolling them up. She calls "They are ready."

The old man shuffles in dragging his left leg with his left arm hanging by his side. He pushes the kitchen door open restricting the space and stands in front of the girl. She turns to pass him a plate. Ignoring this he presses against her and runs his hand softly up her thigh. Her face registers confusion, then shock before she gathers herself and laughing nervously tries to pass him. It is impossible.

As she tries to free herself he says, "Tick Tock, take your time, tick tock, remember the clock, tick tock," whilst wagging his index finger like a very slow metronome. He picks up one of the plates and turns to take it back into the other room. She picks up the remaining two and follows him as instructed at a slow pace. "Take your time, take your time, tick- tock take your time."

The young girl jumps up from the hardbacked chair as soon as the theme tune to *Dixon of Dock Green* starts to play and says it is time for her to go.

"Wait a moment. I will see you to the bus stop," says the old man.

The girl sits down again looking agitated as he slowly puts on his leather jerkin and beret kept on the hook on the back door. He opens the door and she shoots past him, descends the stairs and waits at the bottom as he navigates the steps with exaggerated care, leaning heavily on the rail.

As they walk the short distance along Albert Road and cross over to Slade Lane, Mr. Rackham decorously touches his beret and smiles as they pass Mrs. Monks and then Mr. Saunders making his way to his Austin A35 parked outside his shop. They stand at the 169 bus stop in silence until the bus is visible around the corner. He seizes his opportunity to cup her face in his hands and lift it up before placing a long, wet kiss on her mouth. She looks out of the corner of her eye like a horse looking to bolt as the bus pulls into the stop, breaks loose, jumps on the back of the bus gives him a smile and a cheery wave, "Goodbye."

9

THE DAY EVERYTHING CHANGES

My best friend Karen and I paid 10/6 each for a ticket to see The Beatles at the Ardwick Apollo on 20th November 1963. It was an evening of heightened emotion. Two and a half thousand of us flooded into the charged atmosphere of the auditorium. The sense of anticipation built until we were all into herd mentality. The Beatles burst on with *Please Please Me* and by the time they had got to *Twist and Shout*, the screaming was so loud that you could hear nothing except the booming bass line and the blood-rushing in your ears. Girls were fainting, crying and in truth experiencing something that I, for one, could not quite work out. A thirteen-year-old virgin had no idea what sexual arousal felt like, but that was indeed what it was - but it was also far more than that. It was the night that I left behind the biddable little girl and began to question everything that had been my life up until now.

It is a cliché, but there is no better simile to illustrate the change from the 1950's to the 1960's than that of the black and white film bursting into technicolor. Kitchen sink drama then to pop art and psychedelia.

When we emerged from the venue we were like a fluid stunned amalgam of bodies merged into one entity . So dazed was I that I let the sea of people separate me from my pal and wash me up on its periphery. I was saved by the unfathomable luck of Karen's mother who spotted me through the crowd and grabbed me. I remember we were speechless and exhausted, lost in our own thoughts all the way home.

10

THE SWINGING DOOR

We started to hang out at a café called *The Swinging Door*. I got the 169 bus from Albert Road to Lapwing Lane and then walked down Barlow Moor Road. The tiny little café was never meant to hold the multitude of teenagers determined to cram in there, each making one coke last the whole night. Mr. and Mrs. Salieh, the owners, would periodically have to get tough and cull the herd, so that it spilled out onto the pavement .

Us Levenshulme Grammar School girls, Burnage Grammar boys and the local Didsbury teenagers wore a uniform of either parkas, or full-length suede coats, flared jeans often frayed at the hem and platform shoes. Some of the older boys had Vespa scooters and cars which us girls waited to be invited to share. The word "party" would be shouted and there would be an exodus to some- one or other's flat on Landsdowne or Clyde Road. The cooler amongst us would skin up and share a joint.

Couples would find dark corners to explore each other. Some would have guitars on their backs Bob Dylan style. Being around fourteen at this time I fell into the hangers on group. By the time I was fifteen I had risen in status and a group of us broke off and graduated to the Cona Coffee Bar in central Manchester, from where we became aware of *The Twisted Wheel* in Brazennose Street.

11

MANTAX

I had by now gone up in the world as regards employment. I had lied about my age and landed a job for *Mantax* dispatching black cabs on a Sunday 8 am. until. 8 pm. for which I was paid £4. It was a fortune and in truth I would have done it for nothing. Answering the phones was tedious, taking down people's addresses but more often reassuring them that "It was on the way" or as a last resort having to explain to people in a patronising tone that we were only a broadcaster, we did not own the cabs, and therefore could not force one to pick them up. Sitting in the dispatch booth however gave me a buzz I had never felt before. At the end of the shift three words "Redhill Street control" would cause the airways to scream and jam as drivers fought to be the one to pick up the dispatcher from outside. Not only was there the adrenalin of broadcasting but the beginnings of feeling one had *fans.*

The office was on the eighth floor of a disused mill on Redhill Street, Ancoats, right by the canal. Most of the dark satanic building was derelict. The old service lift shook rattled and vibrated its way up to the top and taking it was an act of faith. There was no other way to get to the office. The toilets were out of the office across the huge expanse that had been once been filled with clanking looms and chattering girls. They were unsanitary, antiquated and often home to the proverbial *shit-house rat.* In the winter the weather would blow in through the broken windows like some Dickensian scene. If the call of nature became too pressing to ignore, going to the *lav* was an exercise to be undertaken at great speed. Always glad to get back into the warmth of the office that would be where you would pull up your knickers and rearrange your clothing properly. This oasis in the midst of the dimensional anomaly lurking back into the 1890's, I accepted as just part of the deal. The only thing that mattered to me was getting in that broadcasting Booth.

12

THE TWISTED WHEEL

We started to go to the All-nighters at the *Twisted Wheel*. I would get the 95 bus to Piccadilly Station where we would all meet up and score some uppers. We would have told our parents that we were sleeping at each other's houses. No one ever seemed to check up on this. I think that our parents had somehow sensed that there was something going on that they didn't really want to question. "Your sons and your daughters are beyond your command," I would never tire of singing within earshot of my parents.

I met a boy called Barry there and we shared a love of dancing. He would pick me up in his car and drive into town. The excitement I felt whilst he and I waited in the queue to show our wheel-shaped membership cards filled me with energy. As soon as we were inside we would head through the arches that separated the rooms and up onto the stage area where we whirled and spun and slid our feet along their sides in unison on the talcum powdered floor mouthing the words to the songs.

"She's a little piece of leather, an she's well put together, yeah."

Or "You didn't have to shake it like you did, but you did, yes you did, And I thank you."

We would see Freddie and the Dreamers, Wayne Fontana and The Mindbenders, The Hollies, Joe Cocker, Geno Washington and the Ram Jam Band, Zoot Money, Alexis Korner, John Lee Hooker, Chris Farlowe, and The Who. Long John Baldry was a favourite - he used to have to stoop to stand on the stage. He often had Rod Stewart with him and he sometimes allowed him to sing. There was no separation. No barrier. No *them* and *us*. We all mingled together.

It was all new. All exciting, and all consuming. I ate it, breathed it, and slept it.

My father would say, "Our Cathy, she was such a lovely little girl. She went to see them Beatles and it was as if Old Nick got into her. She is beyond parental control. We will have to have her made a ward of court if this carries on."

I didn't much care. I had lost all respect for my parents. I saw them clearly now, as people with whom I shared absolutely no opinions or values. I had worked out that if I thought and did the approximate opposite of what they said I might be somewhere around the right mark.

13

MANTAX BLACKPOOL CHARITY TRIP

By summer of 1967 I had grown in confidence. I had grown out the cropped hair from my *Mod* period and went to *Eileen* on West Point to have it backcombed and lacquered into a French pleat. I wore Mary Quant false eyelashes and put panstick on my lips. I probably weighed less than eight stone, but then that was not unusual.

I accepted an invitation from *Orange Two*, one of the cab drivers who had made himself available to me on a regular basis. We had slipped into a system where whenever there was an exceptionally lucrative job phoned

in I would say " MRU (message received and understood), Orange Two."
Even though he had not called in.

If he was slow to catch on I would then say, "Yes, go ahead, Orange Two."
And this was his signal to go to a phone box and call in so I could slip him
the details.

He invited me to accompany him on the Annual Manchester Taxi driver's
charity outing for the disabled to Blackpool Pleasure Beach.

I went to *Estelle Modes* on Stockport Road and bought myself an
expensive silk empire-line dress with a red and green floral print, then set
about raising it from knee length to mini length. I often made myself
outfits, more theatrical than practical and wore them with a pair of red
tap shoes that were in fact a size too small. The look I wanted to achieve
was far more important to me than any discomfort, and there was
certainly no thought at all given to any permanent damage that might be
being caused. I would sew all day and into the night in my bedroom
listening to *Radio Caroline*. I remember hearing the first song played on
the station back in 1964, *Not Fade Away* and loving the feeling of being
included in something so anti-establishment.

Orange two, aka Arthur picked me up in his cab decorated with streamer
and balloons and Jack and Dot proudly waved me off. I wish I could
remember all the details of the two handicapped children we picked up
and took on the trip, but in truth I was more interested in starring in this
little show. I felt sure that once Jimmy Savile set eyes upon me I would be
plucked from obscurity into the limelight. I had seen him and his side-
kick, Dave Eagar at the *Top Ten Club* at Belle Vue spinning discs on the
twin turn tables. I had seen Jimmy's Rolls Royce parked outside or
sometimes the little bubble car used to transport this man of
contradictions. I had been there when the revolving stage had revealed
The Rolling Stones. I had seen Little Stevie Wonder led on to the stage. I
felt that this was the world to which I belonged, not the working class
enclave I occupied in Levenshulme.

When we got to Blackpool Jimmy was greeting each cab in turn dressed
in a tracksuit teamed with clunking gold chains and his hair dyed half
blond and half black. His hair was frizzy and broken and over processed
and all in all I found him an utter disappointment, which is just as well as

he never gave me a second glance. Oh well. I thought. " His loss."

14

DOG DAYS WITH JACK 'N' DOT

The highlight of my day was when Arthur gave me the keys to the taxi and I drove it back from Blackpool, just having passed my driving test.

There had been no alcohol at the *Swinging Door*, The *Cona Coffee Bar* or *The Twisted Wheel*. There had been uppers and the odd spliff. From 1966 I had been part of the local gang that used to hang out in West Point Park. We would sometimes go to *The Bluebell* pub or *Browns Dance Hall* both of which were on Stockport Road. I was introduced to vodka and lime and there was a local boy whom I found interesting who wore purple satin shirts and played air guitar along to Jimi Hendrix *Purple Haze.*

I spent time with my friend Karen at her house in Didsbury, where we played the Beatles on the *Dansette* record player in her bedroom. I also spent time with another friend Hilary with whom I had a half share in a horse. He was called *Kinky*, as in the boots, the word conveying nothing else to us at all. We kept *Kinky* along with another horse that she had called *Teddy* in the double stable at her aunt's cottage in Bramhall. *Damery Cottage*, Damery Lane took an hour to get to on the bus from Levenshulme. It was another world. Dosh, Hilary's aunt was a partner in Hilary's father's dental practice on Wilmslow road. She was a glamorous independent woman who lived alone by choice and always had an over-spilling fruit bowl in the centre of her highly-polished table. When she did go out it was to the opera or theatre with professors or consultants. I didn't invite either of them to my house for fear that Jack would insult them believing them to be stuck up. Mind you the local gang were not welcome either as Jack and Dot thought them beneath us. They would call for me at the front gate and I would slip out quickly before there was any chance of them hearing him saying "It's like a bitch on heat - she'll end up in a council house with loads of kids."

My father's mother Annie, lived with us briefly. She had had a cerebral hemorrhage and her short-term memory had gone. She wore bombazine black with a choker around her neck on which she had a cameo. She would go upstairs to the bathroom and before the cistern had refilled she would be making her way up there again. She spoke to Jack as if he were still her little boy chastising him or praising him indulgently. He set up an electric fire with just the bulb lighting up the log effect and placed his mother in front of this with a piece of bread on a fork. She was soon dispatched to a home until her kidneys failed and she went into hospital to die. Jack often told of how he had been invited to view her when she had passed and how no-one had prepared him for the fact that she had turned blue.

Jack hated *Wogs*, *Yids*, Irish, *Spicks*, *Frogs*, *Toffs*, *Spivs*, *Pikies*, snobs, common people, grandmas of the maternal kind, teenagers, my sisters and now me. Many a phone call I received would be ended abruptly by Jack snatching the phone from my hand, slamming it onto the receiver and dragging me away by the arm.

Any attempt I made to discuss with for instance how Bob Dylan had been heckled at the Free trade Hall by purists who felt betrayed by his having *gone electric*, were met with remarks like "We're not interested in that rubbish."

My mother ridiculed the way I sang along to *The Small Faces* song, "It's all too beautiful" elongating the diphthong ridiculously. When Phil, of the purple shirt, broke my heart and I sat at the piano playing just the right-hand part of *Yesterday*, my father laughed and said I was like a lovesick cow. Things were not good. To make matters worse I had lost my job at Mantax and so was no longer *paying my way*. Someone had rumbled my little wrinkle with Orange Two.

I was in the sixth form now and I was doing A level English, Art and Biology and thought I might perhaps become a games teacher, that being the only option the careers woman had felt appropriate.

All this was to become irrelevant the final night when Jack and I had a set to and I found myself looking for a flat.

15

PICTURE THIS FIGHT WITH JACK

Jack and Dot are asleep in bed, when they are woken by a loud bang followed by the sound of tinkling glass.

"What the bloody 'ell"

"I don't know! maybe its outside"

"No, it's not, It's 'er! What the bloody 'ell is going on?"

" Leave it Jack, its nothing leave it "

"That's not nothing! What's that silly little bitch up to?"

"I'll go Jack "

"No you bloody won't. I'll sort this out."

He pulls on his pants and descends the stairs.

In the kitchen the teenaged girl is on her knees picking up broken glass from the floor.

The stew that Dot had left in the Pyrex dish, standing on an asbestos mat on a low light has splattered its contents up the wall behind the cooker. Brown gravy drips and runs down the tiles. The girl has an amused look on her face as she gets to her feet and turns to explain.

"I turned the heat up too high, and it exploded. I'm sorry, I'll clean it up."

"You're sorry are you? Well you will be."

She bursts into laughter

"Have you been drinking?"

Before she can answer he catches her off-guard with a blow to the side of the head, and as she reels from the impact and turns her head, he slaps her across the other side of her face. She staggers backwards and falls against the bottom stair, its metal edging hitting her lower back causing her to crumple like a wrestler hitting the ropes. Jack takes hold of her by the hair and throws her across the room.

Dot who has been trying to get down the stairs passes into the corner of the kitchen and implores, "Stop it Jack. Oh, please stop, Jack!" as she wrings her handkerchief in her hand.

Jack is hearing nothing. " Laugh at me would you? You little bitch, you're drunk!"

At this moment an animal scream comes from the girl and she runs at him kicking, biting and hammering his chest with her fists.

" Stop it you two, you're like Kilkenny cats. Stop it" Dot dabs at her eyes with the handkerchief.

The girl delivers a kick to his groin and Jack doubles up as she makes for the stairs. She runs up them two at a time, with Jack close behind grabbing for her ankles. She slides open the bathroom door, whizzes it shut and locks it behind her just as Jack reaches it trying to pull it open.

"I can wait! You can't stay in there all night; you've got to come out some time "

She pulls the towels from the rail, makes a makeshift pillow and lies down on the bathroom floor. She is bleeding and bruised. So is Jack.

Dot helps him back to the bedroom, where he sinks down onto the bed.

Meanwhile his fourth daughter lies on the bathroom floor hyperventilating in a pool of urine.

16

WITHINGTON

Its late autumn 1967. My new friend - I shall call her Pen - opens the door to our flat for one, to her parents. Her mother is unloading jars of apple puree and egg custard from her basket.

Pen's father is saying, "I will pay the rent this time, Penelope. I don't know what you have done with the money we gave you. I'm not sure about all this at all. This modelling business, it's not a proper career is it? I don't know why you can't take a job in the council with prospects and a structure."

"She has to try Dan; she did win after all. Lots of girls would love a chance to be a model," says Pen's mum.

Pen says nothing. She has no intention of prolonging this visit. She has things to do. She smiles at her daddy, takes the money, kisses him on the cheek and soon they are gone. Pen, from the Wirral had won a competition in the *Liverpool Echo* the prize being a modelling course at *The Lucy Clayton Model Agency*.

After I had put my father in bed from his injuries, my mother had told me I would have to move out. He would no longer have me in the house. I had found Pen through an advertisement in the *Manchester Evening News* and the two of us moved in to the tiny flat in Withington. I had managed the first month's rent and then got myself a job selling stretch covers for a man with a shop in Stockport. He was some ten year older than us and by chance was a male model.

Pen had found out from her fellow models in Manchester that *Blinkers Nightclub* was the place to go. We had managed to move a second single bed into the flat but on this particular evening we had got into one bed together to keep warm before putting on one bar of the electric fire, putting on our *gladrags* and getting the bus in to town. We joined the queue on the corner of King Street West and were admitted without hesitation from the doorman Stephen.

We walked down the stairs to be greeted by Selwn Demmy saying, "Well hello girls. Haven't seen you here before. Welcome. This is your club."

He ushered us in and the first person we saw standing at the bar was George Best.

George was surrounded by his entourage and his best friend and hairdresser Malcolm bought us a drink. We danced and drank the night away until the lights came up and the signature tune of *Goodnight Blinkers* was played. We didn't have money for a taxi and hadn't given any thought to how we would get home, so it was fortuitous that George and Pen took off together in his *E-Type* and Malcom dutifully offered me a lift home.

We had little money and even less to eat. Pen's best friend from the

Wirral, Val, brought us tins of green beans and tins of chicken in white sauce from Marks & Spencer, whom her father supplied with fruit and veg. Pen had splashed out £2.10d shillings on a mongrel terrier from Tib Street, even though they had had dogs from £1 each. She named him *Dennis*. He ate when and what we did. Pen was off with George most nights and at the week-ends I would be invited along to the *Fifth Inn Restaurant*. Pen and I would peruse the menu like connoisseurs.

"Ooo fish," Pen might deliberate. "Hmmm...I'd love some fish."

In truth we were so hungry we could have eaten the menu. George, Malcolm and pals usually had prawn cocktail, Steak Diane, and Black Forest Gateau washed down with either Mateus Rose or Liebfraumilch, so I followed suit.

On Sundays there was a social gathering at Selwyn Demmy's flat at Appleby Lodge where we all hung out and would be plied with booze and food. Dennis came along with us and ate what was left over. One of our funny stories was of how George would take *Dennis* with him training and how he had confused Dennis Law by shouting "Come on Denise, get your nose out of there."

If George brought us food from *the Chippy* as he often did, Pen and I would get fish 'n' chips whilst *Dennis* got chicken, for some reason best known to Mr. Best.

We lived a life of extremes. One minute I would be standing shivering at the bus stop waiting to get the bus to work in Stockport in my red slingbacks in the snow. The next would see us being driven around in E-Types being wined and dined. Every month Pen's dad said it was the last month he would pay the rent. I was more worried about this than Pen, as without her I would be sunk.

17

MAYFAIR MANSIONS

Pen *graduated* from *Lucy Clayton* and was more interested in spending time with George than going on assignments. She was offered a job on the cloak room at *Blinkers* and met two other girls who were interested in sharing a flat with us so we moved from our flat off Wilbraham road into an eccentrically large apartment in what had been, at the turn of the century, The Italian Consulate. This was Mayfair Mansions, Mersey Road, Didsbury a building owned by the Gyles family.

Marjorie Gyles was a producer at Granada TV Studios and had a flat off to the left of the grand entrance hall. She had a long-term thing going with the barrister Lionel Cohen who lived in the garden ground-floor flat and we moved into the *Oak Flat* which had steps down from the lounge onto the front lawn. Lionel had been passed over for silk many times due to his reputation for drink and debauchery. Although Marjorie was probably a great match for him both socially and intellectually, she was one of those women who have a top of small proportions and the bottom belonging to an elephant. Lionel toed the line just enough for her to forget when his rent was due and to have him escort her to functions. When he had drunk sufficient whisky in his own flat he would knock on our front door, be let in by one of us, not wishing to cause offense, and take to wandering about from bed to bed trying to get in with one or other of us.

The flat was eccentric in as much as it had a kitchen and dining room, an oak-paneled, large formal room with a walk-in fireplace, one bedroom and a dark passageway along to an Arctic bathroom. It had obviously been built as a reception suite not a flat. Pen slept in the bedroom, usually with George, who spent little time at his lodgings in Chorlton at Mrs. Fullaway's. Jan and Cary slept in opposite corners of the main room and I in the partitioned off half of the kitchen.

Dennis did as he pleased. He would follow us and board the bus, sitting next to us on the seat smiling and wagging as whichever one of us it happened to be tried to deny all knowledge of him.

A *Wella* Representative about his business, who was part of our crowd, had pulled up at the lights at Barlow Moor Road in his Cortina one summer's day, with his window wound down only to find *Dennis* jumping in to join him. *Dennis* was a true dog of the sixties.

It was odd for me to be back in the vicinity of the *Swinging Door* again where I could see my younger self hanging about on the pavement of the shops which were now our locals.

Next to the end of the black and white parade of shops was a ladies top end clothes shop called *Judith Taylor*. It was a shop we all aspired to but could only afford at sale time. Judith herself always beautifully dressed and had that timeless look one still sees nowadays - a blunt heavily fringed bob, high cheek-bones, long lashes and a full mouth. She had two daughters by a renowned bad boy called Miles Baddeley. He had a shop called *Seven Miles Out* on the main road out of Stockport. He had a tame leopard on a chain that accompanied him everywhere, even sitting in his car on the front passenger seat. Judith and Miles had had a brief sparky marriage and then she had dumped him as he was too much to handle. He seemed to still be in love with her. Not in love enough to behave though, as I found to my cost one day when I ventured into his *Emporium* only to be locked in and chased around the shop.

By Spring 1968 I had witnessed how much the modelling paid both Pen and John, the man whose shop I ran in Stockport. I figured I could earn as much in one day modelling as I got paid for the week. A new business called the *Pam Holt Agency"* had splintered from *Lucie Clayton's* so I joined that.

For the next three years we lived this hedonistic, communal hand to mouth existence. Probably the best years of our lives if only we had known that.

The end of the sixties saw the age of Woodstock together with all its Love Peace and optimism change metaphorically into Altamont where the Hells Angels security and the changing climate brought about death and disillusionment during the Rolling Stones set at the Free Festival. I had no conception of the fact that everything must always be in a state of change. We were too busy living in the here and now.

Cath's mother

Fanny Lillian and Timothy McCarthy

80 Albert Road

Dot and Cath

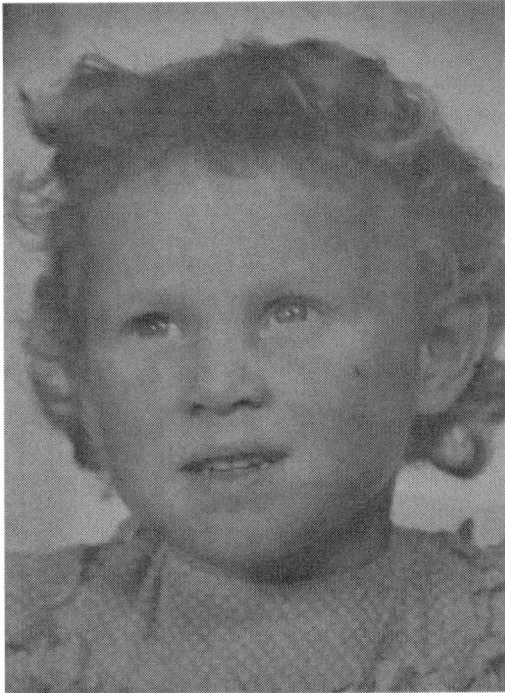
Little Cath aged 4

Stockport Road 1950s

J.Mawson Plumbers Shop

Osbourne Road

Jack and Dot

Mayfair Mansions

Cath and Peter's wedding day 1971

Cath 1969

Cath 1970

18

PICTURE THIS DR HOOK

Dr Hook and the Medicine Show play Manchester.

After the show the current trendy hot-spot is kept open after hours for them and the in-crowd. At the Bar they stand alongside George Best, his disciples and their female interests. The night wears on, drinks flow, drugs are taken, and the conversation is getting sloppy.

Dennis, the guitarist, turns to the young woman standing next to him. She has a clip-on hairpiece and thick false eyelashes and wears a Mary Quant mini-dress with white lacy plastic boots. She appears to be unattached and so he makes his clumsy move on her. She, emboldened by various mind- altering substances, throws a drink in his face. He rushes to the kitchen, picks up the slops bucket from the floor, runs it under the cold water tap and comes back around to the front of the bar. He swings back the bucket, ready to throw it over the girl.

George and his friend Frank link the girl's arms, one standing either side of her.

"OK you throw it," says Frank "but if it goes over her it goes over us too. I'd give that some thought mate, if I was you."

Dennis puts down the bucket and turns his back.

Through my drunken haze it registers. "Phew, that was a close one. Why on earth did I do that?"

19

GEORGE BEST

1I had no real clue what a big deal George was. Of course, we knew that when he had stayed at our flat in Withington having parked his car in the back, there would be a crowd of mainly girls surrounding the place when we were trying to leave the next morning, but we knew nothing at all about football.

When Pen and I had moved from the Withington flat to the Didsbury place, George had hidden under the bed clothes on one of the beds in the main room and when the removal men entered bringing in our belongings, he popped up and they went completely to pieces. I don't know what he and Pen talked about when on their own but I never had a meaningful conversation with him at all in all that time. That wasn't unusual though. We didn't bother with the News, the government, religion, politics, philosophy or indeed anything other than music, going out, clothes, and strutting our stuff.

Years later, after George had moved to London, I encountered him coming out of *Horts Wine Bar* in St Ann's Square. He seemed pleased to see me and suggested going back in for a drink. We sat at the bar and were soon joined by a man called Nobby Carstairs, who wrote material for people including the Lancashire comedian and singer, Mike Harding.

Nobby was always around and was something of a court jester. He was funny without meaning to be sometimes. For example, when I bumped into him coming out of Tescos in Didsbury he told me in all seriousness that he had not bought any eggs due to his concerns about the listeria problem at the time. When I pointed out the glaring inconsistency of the fact that I could see he had bought two cartons of two hundred fags and a bottle of whisky he was slow to see the humour.

He made a beeline for George and myself offering to buy us drinks. I opted for a dry white wine and George said grinning, " I'll have to start with lager. I've got this bloody thing put in my stomach and if I go straight on to vodka it makes me throw up."

This was also funny, if it hadn't been so tragic.

Nobby put down a ten-pound note on the bar, and when the barman went to pick it up, he pulled the piece of wire to which it was attached and the note skittered away. It was one of his trademark moves. Nobody bothered too much about the payment of the bill as was often the case where George was concerned. It was dark when we fell out of the bar and into taxis from the rank outside. I had had a more meaningful conversation with George that day than in all the time back in the late

60's.

Pen found out that her time was up when Eva Haraldsted arrived on the scene. The first thing I noticed about Eva was a hairstyle I had never seen before. She had so much hair that the top portion was held in a kind of loose pinned ponytail and the rest hung down her back. She and George were inseparable, which made it hard for Pen as we were involved in playing a charity football match under the name of *Blinkers United* at this time and Eva immediately took pride of place .They quickly became engaged before George just as quickly changed his mind and it was over. I seem to remember his next girlfriend being Toni Ceo who moved her children and goods over from the United States and ended up being dumped in a hotel in Alderley Edge.

Eva stayed around and started to date the *Wella* Representative, the one who Dennis had joined in his car. One night we were all in *Blinkers* and when they walked in George got the D.J. to play *Get Back* by The Beatles repeatedly. Eva's suitor jumped into the raised booth and knocked the needle off the record.

Paddy Crerand, normally a quiet gentle family man, punched Chris, Eva's beau, and broke his jaw. He was carted out and the evening continued just as normal.

20

MARRIAGE

Late summer 1971 saw me getting married. Pen and Jan moved to London, and Cary to Redhill to become an air hostess . The end of an era.

On the day of my wedding Jack stopped the car and said

"There's only one thing worse you could have done to me our Cath, and that's marry a wog!"

Trying to keep myself together I replied, "Just listen to yourself; you are a disgrace"

"I'm just telling you that I am against this."

"Well, thank you for that insight and wisdom."

"I'm just telling you; on your own head be it"

"Well, that much I know. However will I manage without all your support? Now if you please, just drive."

That is how the father of the bride delivered her to the Registrar's Office in central Manchester that day in late August 1971 on only the second time I had seen my parents since 1967.

There was no way to reason with Jack. When I had pointed out that unlike himself who had found himself a reserved occupation during the war, my future husband's father, even though Jewish and therefore if taken prisoner facing terrible consequences, had in fact been a commando. A commando praised for his bravery and leadership and not a spiv as Jack thought all Jews were. Jack had been a member of Mosley's black shirts.

Cyril and Betty, Peter's parents, had been a golden couple, had a thriving business, lived in a splendid house and had four children, two boys and two girls. Betty died from cancer on my future husbands 18th birthday. Peter had been in Switzerland when he received the call, on a course at the Longines watch company.

Cyril had been devasted and whilst doing his best to look after his family was in a bad way. His business had failed after he had ploughed into it the money from the house sale, and he and his brood now lived courtesy of another branch of the family in a flat in West Didsbury. Cyril was chain smoking and drinking whisky to numb his pain.

Peter and I had no idea of who we were or what we expected of each other. Peter needed mothering and I needed protection. We did alright for the first couple of years. I was earning good money and we were bailed out by Cyril when we got into difficulties. However, when our daughter was born two years later and I stayed at home, we hit the rocks. Had we realised I had ambition and Peter was happier at home things might have been different. There was no advice from distracted Cyril and certainly none from my family. He could have become a house husband and I could have been the bread winner. We got into terrible financial difficulties and were headed for bankruptcy and I decided that I would be better on my own.

The bank was trying to take our house, there was a second mortgage it seemed and no tax had been paid. I took in two lodgers, found a child minder in East Didsbury and set about finding work. That year I ended up as the second highest earner on the Agency's books and was also part of a team who did up to three evening fashion shows a week for boutiques in the greater Manchester area.

And my friend Barbara got me an equity card through her cousin who had a dance school in Liverpool. This meant that I could do extra work at Granada Studios on Quay Street. Things were happening again.

21

PICTURE THIS JACK AND DOT

The little car turns down the un-made-up road and pulls into the driveway of the partly built bungalow, on the left-hand side, the last plot before the sea. She is met by a man in overalls, in his sixties and still muscular.

"I've been waiting for you. I expected you sooner. Where's yer mother? Dot! Our Cath's here! God knows where she gets to. Let me show ye. Luke at all these bricks. I've ad te move them all meself. Dot! Where is she? Yes, there aren't many men my age could be doing this."

Dot appears from around the back, surreptitiously popping a polo mint into her mouth. She wears an apron over her crimplene slacks and lace up shoes. She smiles with her mouth but her eyes are blank. "I'm coming Jack! I don't know; your life's not your own around here. You have to drop everything whenever you are summoned. Hello luv How are you? Do you want a cup of tea?"

The young woman is led off for a further tour of the building site. Dot is left to drag chairs and a table into the sun and fetch the tea on unsteady legs.

Jack is lifting up a window frame from a stack of them to show how and where it will be fixed into the building when there is a crash. Jack and Catherine run to the spot where Dot is standing looking at the dropped tea tray and its broken contents scattered on the ground.

"This ground is so uneven. Its bloody dangerous around here. Watch yourself won't you!"

Dot bends over to clear up the mess but over balances and breaks wind unexpectedly as she topples over. Everyone pretends not to notice. Catherine sees that Dot's shoes are worn down on the outside of the heels and somehow this makes tears spring to her eyes. She scoops up the debris, takes it into the makeshift kitchen, leaving the others to gather themselves in hushed raised voices. She returns with a much simpler presentation of three mugs already filled with tea.

They sit down at the table. Catherine distributes the tea whilst Dot fumbles trying to free a saccharin tablet from its dispenser.

"I have come with great news," says Catherine.

Jack and Dot say nothing.

"Yes...I've come to tell you that I am pregnant" she says beaming. Jack looks at her with a glint in his eye. Dot looks away.

"Don't expect me to enthuse about the thoughts of another little yid coming into this world," spits Jack.

Catherine pushes back her chair, picks up her handbag, jumps into the car, backs it down the drive and as she hits the accelerator to screech off she sees in her rear-view mirror Dot running after the car shouting, "Come back; please don't go. Come back".

22

THE 70s

What to say about the seventies? Sexism was a given. It was a decade where I made my money from photographic work for catalogues such as *Great Universal, Damart, Babette, Littlewoods* and Wynne Walsh's weekly fashion column in the *Manchester Evening News*. I did catwalk modelling for *Bernshaw, Shubette, The Way In, Alexon*, and *Mondi*. I was on *Kellogg's* packets, in holiday brochures, carpet adverts and DIY catalogues. The work came thick and fast. Exhibitions selling everything from kitchen gadgets to cars, motor bikes to boats, all sold with the aid of *tits and bums*.

Television offered no respite. The first job I had was in *Coronation Street*. I was to play a Bunny Girl type waitress. In the plot *Stan Ogden*, working at the time as The Lord Mayors chauffeur, had taken the car without permission and for some reason ended up in an up-market kind of club.

The scene opened with the obligatory panning shot up my legs. I walked down a stairway carrying the drinks to a table at which Stan and some others, in on the joy ride, including *Elsie Tanner* were seated. After a few takes of this Pat Phoenix proclaimed loudly, "One begins to wonder who is the star around here. One can only hope that she goes arse over tit."

I pretended not to have heard, gave it my best shot and melted back into the background, as extras do.

My next role was that of *Girl in hot-pants* in The Lovers. The running gag was that, as *Geoffrey Bubbles Bon-Bon,* Richard Beckinsale was trying to get a simpering Paula Wilcox into bed while she was set on marriage. Her mind was focused on setting up home and his was on getting laid. Every time he had been caught out in some kind of impure motivation and had sworn to try to do better, I would walk past and he would give me a long and lingering look, usually over her shoulder, whilst reassuring her that he was to be trusted.

I began to get bits with lines.

"Star time! Courtesy of Mr. Ricky Lamont," I announced loudly in a mid-Atlantic accent, only to revert to "ere, d' you want this piccy took 'r what!" when the group were slow to strike a pose. I was playing a free-lance photographer in something called *Send in the Girls* The free-lance photographer was again scantily clad. I never questioned the why's and wherefores.

I had a good run in period dramas. *The Victorians* meant no make-up, lots of ringlets and a full crinoline.

I had been booked for this week of work along with the friend who had got me my equity card and Val Martin, who had been Miss Something or other.

Val was known for wearing skin-tight, hip-hugging, white flared pants.

Her dancing to Marvin Gaye's *I Heard It Through The Grapevine* was renowned in *Blinkers*. She would could sway from side to side, the top half of her body facing one way, the bottom part, the opposite, whilst lowering her knees almost to the floor before shimmying back up again. I had had the honour of her lending me the pattern from which she cut and sewed her pants, but I didn't feel I carried them of as well as she did. They were, after all from a pattern adapted completely for her body, not mine. She smoked Black Russian cigarillos and it was a wonderfully incongruous sight to see this Victorian shrinking violet lighting up, between takes.

One of the long scenes we were involved in was a ball. Val was coupled with a strange little bald man who made a living reading from Dickens and came up to her décolletage. We were doing a polka and I swear his feet left the ground at every swirl.

Granada was a hotbed of talent in the seventies. Everyone would be crammed into the canteen together and you'd be squeezing past pop groups in the corridors. One time we were in the next dressing room to *The Bay City Rollers* and had to be hustled out through the crowds outside to get to our cars.

It was during one of my tea-breaks in full costume that I was joined at my table by *The Kinks*. Ray Davies struck up a conversation with me leading to an invitation to join him later that evening. I considered myself to be quite cool, but on this occasion I found myself completely dumbstruck and couldn't even lift my teacup from its saucer my hands were shaking so much. I made an excuse and ran off calling myself all kinds of cowardly alliterative swearwords under my breath.

23

BRIDESHEAD

At this time Brideshead Revisited was being filmed out on location at Castle Howard. It was a long booking and us extras were picked up at some God-awful hour outside Granada and taken out there on a coach.

We wore the most amazing flapper dresses which became more compromised every day, unable to withstand the punishing regime. The story line was of a huge party populated by the black jazz musicians and flapper society of the 1920's. It was being directed by Michael Lindsay-Hogg who had a successful play on Broadway at the time and was commuting between here and New York.

I was given a partner for the whole of the shoot called Michael who was part of a group of black musicians brought in from the London School of Music. We got on really well and he was talented and fascinating. There was a room at Castle Howard that was circular and could only hold around twelve people at a time. One of the days Michael and I were directed to walk past the entrance to this room as three of the main characters were talking on the bed. Michael Lindsay-Hogg called Michael and myself over in between takes, and offered us an upgrade.

"Ok. What are your names? Right, Michael and Catherine, what I want you to do is this. I want you to take off your clothes and simulate sex on the bed behind these guys. We will give you some dialogue. Go see my assistant, give her your names and she will draw up your contract, ok?. Right everybody, That's a wrap for today. Ten o clock sharp tomorrow. Thank you everyone."

I left for home feeling elated. I knew enough to know that Brideshead Revisited was a classic and that Michael Lindsay-Hogg was big league. This could be important.

24

KEITH

In the late seventies I was seeing Keith. His father and half-brother had left behind their roots in Wythenshawe and were so nouveaux riche one could still see *the grabbing*. Cliff, Keith's father had been given the job of disposing of World War Two surplus from a huge hangar outside Liverpool. This he unashamedly described as having carried out on a "One for you, two for me" basis. He had married a widow with three children.

She too was from an impoverished background and it seems her son, Peter, had slept in a drawer as a baby, the luxury of a cot being out of their reach. Peter was a ruthless entrepreneur and made his first fortune selling kitchens direct to the public. The two daughters and their mother were of little influence over Cliff and Peter but Keith, the only child from Joan and Cliff's union, was fast tracked to the top of one of their companies which sold carpets in Scotland and the North.

Keith is best summed up by the following event. One night when he was late home and I had my daughter at my home being cared for, I took the rare opportunity to drive to a club in Fallowfield called *Sandpiper* in which Peter had shares, and was their current, favourite watering hole. As I drove my mini into the car park, I saw Cliff's Rolls Royce parked in a corner and could see people in the back. As I drew level I saw Keith supine, his eyes closed, his mouth stretched in a rapturous grin and activity in the form of a bobbing head in his lap. Horrified, I drove off and went home.

The result of this was a few days of our being incommunicado, which was not unusual in our tempestuous relationship. When we kissed and made up Keith enjoyed delivering his explanation: "Flash, I've been getting blow jobs in the back of Rolls Royces since I was fourteen. It's you what's sat on my roof garden."

I should have walked away but I found him funny, exciting and sexy.

So, back to the night before I was due to take up my opportunity in Brideshead, I mentioned it during the telephone conversation with Keith. His ruling was swift and clear. "Oh really, Flash. Fine then, you do that, but you can then collect all your bits of stuff from my apartment and call it a day. It will be *Goodnight Vienna*."

I put down the phone shocked and outraged.

25
BRIDESHEAD REVISITED

Ten o clock the next day saw me standing in front of our director saying, "I am sorry Mr. Lindsay-Hogg, I can't do this."

Mr. Hogg wore a glove leather blouson, had a sharp haircut and square jawline from which often protruded a chunky cigar. He was a man of vision and few words. Without missing a beat, he turned from us, clicked his fingers at the nearby couple and called them over, leaving Michael and myself to slope off, Michael looking daggers at me.

I had to spend another week partnered with this lovely man who could barely look at me as I had blown his chance and maybe, he would have reasoned, *just maybe she wouldn't do it because I'm black*. I felt this very deeply and regretted my decision. At the time I rationalised it by saying that had I been one of the lead characters I would have done it, but the tiny part I would have had didn't warrant my taking my clothes off.

26

BUGS THAT DRUGS CAN'T BEAT

Ten years later, when I was no longer in the entertainment business, an opportunity presented itself for me to lay the ghost. Someone I knew in the casting business phoned me up to say that they were having difficulty in finding a group of people to work on a serious Panorama programme called *Bugs That Drugs Can't Beat*. It was a prescient look at the superbugs to be found in operating theatres which could not by beaten by antibiotics. They were looking for a group of eight people who represented a cross section of the public, who would appear naked. They were needed as a backdrop to superimpose scientific pictures of microbes and reactions on to, and also to illustrate and bring to life the dialogue. I said I would do it and also recruited my then boyfriend, Mike.

Mike was a fiercely intelligent and well-educated man. He had been a dentist when, " The state of the nation's teeth was so dire that there was a fortune to made, if you were prepared to work your bollocks off," as he put it. He and his partner Jack had done just that. They had bought a piece of land in Ashton, built a clinic and set up a monster National Health Practice. They had worked their bollocks off during the day and at night gone all over the country adding to their property portfolio. They would describe their partnership as one where Mike had the flair and Jack made sure all the *T's* were crossed and the *I's* were dotted

Mike had Crohns Disease. This he attributed to having been brought up by three women dedicated to his wellbeing and keeping all germs away from him so that when he went away to university it came to light that his immune system was not up to par. His father had been killed on the *Burma Road,* and his mother had never remarried. He had been brought up by his grandma, his Auntie Betty and his mother and he would do a wicked impression of them. "Ay awr Mittle, ye'll neva guess what. Ah wer sittin ere this mornin lewkin outta the winder an yew'll neva gess o shud cum a warkin up the gardin path."

Mike was many faceted. He could be as camp as the campest when mixing with the ballet crowd, and as macho as Popeye should an emergency present itself whilst we were sailing. Due to his Crohns he was very slim and had long thin legs.

The eight of us included a black body builder who had a gym on Bridge Street and also had connections in the TV and advertising world. The programme was being put together in a studio in a back street where we spent the next ten days. The first day we all went up to our dressing rooms and put on the white towelling robes supplied .All of us except Mike who had brought his own from home. Mike was put in a dressing room with the body builder and was very funny in playing up the extremes of body type between himself and his room-mate as they walked along together.

The first three days were spent blocking shots and generally working out logistics. On the fourth day we were asked to "drop the dressing gowns" and I remember I gulped and froze initially before mustering the courage to comply. Every day it became more natural to us to be naked. We were old hands by the end giving it no thought at all.

In the height of summer that year, Mike and I were walking along Bridge Street in Manchester when we saw Royston, the body builder, walking towards us on the other side of the road. He wore a bandana and a white vest type tee-shirt under a one piece, red, lycra bib 'n' braces shorts set.

"Hey! Hello there!" shouted Mike over the traffic. "I didn't recognise you with your clothes on."

27

THE FRIAR'S GOOSE

The yacht slips its mooring in the marina in Kusadasi island, Turkey, and is navigated by Mike around the array of other moored boats shining in the bright sunlight reflecting off the clear blue water. A gentle breeze makes a tinkling sound as it blows through their mast equipment.

Mike is thin and sinewy in his white tee-shirt and jeans. His white hair is tied back in a pony-tail, his chin is covered in white stubble and he has a cigarette jammed in the corner of his mouth. Catherine stands on the bow looking down at the white spray bouncing off either side of the boat as it cuts through the water.

Today is the first day out sailing for Catherine and the maiden voyage for Mike's new boat *Friars Goose*. The plan is to make the short crossing to the Greek Island of Samos and to fuel up. Mike had had a smaller fibre-glass *Moody* that he had spent previous years bay-hopping in around the Mediterranean Sea. This is a serious steel ketch just bought from a couple who live in Istanbul and built for crossing oceans. It has been standing unused for quite a while and this will be something of a shake down trip to see how she handles.

Once in the open waters Mike hands the wheel over to Catherine and shows her the course to take. This is her first experience and she is concentrating hard determined to take it all in. Mike gets the sails up but the wind is "all over the place" and after some fiddling about and tacking he decides that they will put the engine back on instead.

He hands the wheel over to Catherine saying casually to turn it to windward. She has no idea what this means but turns the wheel until the sails start to flap and Mike indicates that that is indeed what is required. He starts to lower the sails gathering them up ready to tie them down and Catherine looks around drinking in this new world feeling the sway of the ocean and the heat of the sun on her face.

Suddenly she is startled out of her reverie by Mike shouting, "Fuckin 'ell Cath, turn the wheel. Turn the wheel. You're headed straight for those rocks." His face is a picture of sheer panic, his eyes open wide and his jaw involuntarily dropped. And already he is running along the deck towards her.

She turns the wheel away from the headland and the view from the cockpit changes dizzyingly. Emergency averted but feeling foolish Catherine offers mitigation. "...But you took down the sails! I thought we had stopped."

Mike, never one to resist the opportunity of a *bon mot,* uttered the phrase that Catherine would never forget. "What an amazing mis-conception!"

28

GRANADA TELEVISION

I was a regular at Granada throughout the seventies and took the work as it came. I was booked to play a character called Jilly West in *Coronation Street.* Jilly was a cabaret singer employed in the *Capricorn Club,* where at the time Rita Fairclough was the resident singer. I made a play for her boss and her job but was sent packing by the righteous and wholesome Rita.

I was welcomed into *Coronation Street* by Betty Driver who played Betty Turpin. She advised me conspiratorially to "Tell em nowt" when the publicity person came to interview me. Even Pat Phoenix and I had a few nice chats and I thought it best not to bring up our previous meeting.

All was going swimmingly. I was booked for identity parades in *The Krypton Factor.* I was regularly in something about a Pickles factory starring Hilda Baker and Jimmy Jewel. I was even in items in the local news programmes so I thought nothing of it when I was sent the script to do something with Norman Wisdom. I was to be the usual objectivised *bird* for Norman to play off. What I hadn't envisaged was that this involved his putting his face in my cleavage and jiggling my breasts. When I stepped away from him the attitude from the director was one of incredulity. How on earth could I think there was anything wrong with a bit on innocent fun. Norman was a star, loved by everyone. On a reflex I told the director to stick it and walked out. I received a phone call from the ladies in Wardrobe telling me how proud they were of me and that was exactly how us women should deal with this kind of thing. I was gratified by their response, it is just a pity that this view was not shared by the casting department, as the work dried up.

29
YORKSHIRE TELEVISION

Fortunately for me, my agent started to send me to do little bits at Yorkshire television. It was nowhere near as handy as Granada but I was soon regularly driving up and down the M62. I was picked up by the production team of *321*. I was in sketches that were unfathomable to me. I was there opening fridge doors and gesturing to its features. I was lying on sunbeds. I was wheeled in sitting on king-sized beds wearing sexy nighties. There was a woman called Eve who cleaned and provided teas and coffees at one of the fashion houses at the back of Piccadilly in Manchester where I was a regular in-house model. "EEE Kaate, its te be oped they never give a toilet away on that *321*, else they'll ave yew sat on it!" she astutely and succinctly remarked.

There were two sexist stories doing the rounds of Yorkshire TV at this time. One was about Freddie Star, the other about Paula Yates.

The one about Freddie I heard from more than one of the crew, all of whom were male. It goes like this: "Oh what a lad he is that Freddie! He was here a while ago in a sketch and it involved a woman dressed as a shepherdess complete with hooped skirt and crook. She was singing *Once on a hill stood a lonely goat herd, Layey yodel ayyey jodel ay ety!* through an open window in the backdrop of the set. The studio audience was in and they were going for a take. Freddie sneaked around the back of the set and attempted a rear entry on the woman just as she was doing the yodeling bit. More than one of the crew had perfected their impression of how she had screeched the high note and carried on like a trooper.

The other story was about Paula Yates, a teenager at the time. She had been in the building along with the man she believed to be her father, Jess Yates. He had been doing some *God slot* programme at the time. "Oh what a slut she is. She went through the building from the electricians to the camera men to researchers. They all had her." So they said And what did I say? I said "Hmmmmm" I had learned to be non-committal. It was more beneficial to one's career to say nowt.

Cath 1979: First Series Countdown

Cath with Richard Whiteley and Carol Vorderman

The Countdown Girls

Kenneth Williams with Cath

Leaving day L to R: Richard Whiteley, Cath, Nick Abson, John Mead, Michael Whylie, Carol Vorderman, Graham

Cath and Carol Vorderman

Blinkers United: Back R – Cath, Pen & George Best. Centre front- Eva Haraldsted

Keith and Catherine

Catherine modelling fur coats

Catherine 1981

Catherine on the Friar's Goose at Kusadasi Marina

Cath and Mike

Catherine present day (2020)

30
COUNTDOWN

The call came from my agent that Yorkshire Television were holding an audition for a hostess for a new quiz programme. I drove over to the Hotel in Leeds and sat in the reception area with all the other hopefuls. There were plenty of girls there whom I knew. All clutching our portfolios, we waited our turn. I had recently returned from Spain, was tanned and wore a boob tube, skin tight pink jeans and high heels. When my turn came I stood before the panel made up from the production team and was asked how I was with words. Encouraged that this might be more cerebral than my work up to date I told them words were my forte and I would welcome a chance to shine. They told me that they had done a pilot and were planning to do a series of six programmes funded from the local News programme *Calendar*. It was based on a French programme called *Des Chiffres et des lettres* and was to be called *Calendar Countdown*. The force must have been with me that day, and a few days later I was called to say I had got it and given the details.

A short while later we were on set in the YTV studios. I was introduced to Richard Whitely who was to be mine host and a woman called Denise McFarland-Cruikshanks who was to do the mathematics part of the show. Ted Moult, a TV personality with a farming background. was to sit in part of the set called *Dictionary Corner* along with a representative from the Oxford English Dictionary who was there to check the validity of the words. Richard, I was told by the floor manager was only being used as he was already on the staff so they would not have to pay extra fees to him. It was all very much on a shoe string and I had to supply my own clothes.

We were a friendly little group who worked together to come up with some kind of format. Richard was ill at ease and wooden, I wasn't miked up and wandered in and out of set like it was a home movie and Ted Moult regaled us with rambling pointless anecdotes. The contestants were bewildered, and the studio audience even more so. They had been bussed in from an old people's home and those on the front row asked each other constantly and loudly what was going on whilst eating their packed lunches.

Ted Moult and the woman from the Oxford English Dictionary were *on ear piece* from the gallery and were fed a choice of words to offer up as their selection. The producer was pleased that I could spell them and put them up on the board quickly and that often, towards the end of our stint, I was able to pre-empt what the word would be and have it up on the board in the time that the contestants were given to come up with it. This meant the programmes were cheaper to make as they didn't have to stop tape to set up the shot, or do drop shots that had to be edited in later.

We got the six programmes in the can and all went home. Some short while later I watched them go out on television and oscillated between amusement and embarrassment at the amateurishness of it all.

Imagine my surprise when I received a call saying that the programme had been picked up by *Channel Four* and I was given studio dates later that year to film the first proper series.

Then came the shocking news that our producer had been killed in a terrible accident whilst filming in a helicopter. Time passed and I heard from Sandra the personal assistant that a new producer called John Meade had been given the *Countdown* project but it got to within days of the scheduled filming and I had had no confirmation and no contract.

I had learned that one never chases from a position of weakness, so did nothing. The day before filming was due to start I received a letter from this John Meade thanking me for my past participation and telling me that as the programme was now to have a national profile he had replaced me with Miss Great Britain, a person of higher visibility.

I carried on with my day to day life until two days into filming I received a call in the evening out of the blue. The caller was John Meade, obviously from the bar and obviously not sober .He asked if I would step back in. He said that three days of studio time in and they had very little *in the can*. He told me that he couldn't mike up Miss G.B. as she had a broad Bolton accent and they were having to stop tape in every round so that the floor manager could put up the winning word.

There was much slurring and swearing.

I agreed to be in studio the next day.

When I walked into the dressing room that I was to share with Beverley, Miss G.B., it was obvious that she had no inkling that I had been called in and felt her position to be threatened which indeed it was, as her contract was not renewed for the next series.

We were greatly overstaffed. There were two *vital statisticians* a grandiose title typical of John's grandiose thinking. Beverley and I alternated in putting up the letters but with me doing the reveals and Beverley humiliatingly mute.

John Meade was a little man, who wore built-up shoes. He had a big black moustache and a boyish haircut, a liking for Stetson hats and linen suits. His aroma was that of cigarette smoke and whisky from first thing in the morning. His view of woman was that they were either *brainy* or *crumpet* and left us to muddle through as best we could. He spent his time thinking up unsubtle puns, feeding them down the earpiece of Richard who was forced to deliver them in toe-curlingly embarrassed style.

One particular day Richard repeatedly said, "Hello, good evening and welcome to another edition of Calendar Countdown."

"Cut" said the floor manager.

"Sorry" said Richard.

"Going in ten," said the floor manager. "10. 9. 8. 7. 6. 5. 4. 3. 2.1 and go."

"Good evening and welcome to Calendar Countdown," repeated Richard.

"Cut," said the floor manager. "Going in ten, 10.9.8.7.6.5.4.3.2.1. and go."

"Good evening and welcome to Calendar Countdown," said Richard.

By now there were sniggers from both performers and crew. Poor Richard squirming more with every take. When he did it again he put his head in his hands and said, "Countdown, Countdown, Countdown not Calendar Count down! Why, oh why do I keep saying that?" Then he hung his head.

Everyone who was on earpiece burst into laughter, and quickly shared with the rest of us the joke. When Richard had said "Why oh why do I keep saying that," John Meade had clicked open his link and said "Because you're a cunt."

Ted Moult our friendly farmer tragically shot himself in the head and was replaced by Kenneth Williams. The first time I met Kenneth was in the hospitality room at a lunchtime. He sat down next to me at my table, looked me in the eye and said.

> A nymphomanical girl called Alice
> Once used T.N.T. on her phallus,
> They found her vagina in North Carolina,
> And her arsehole in Buckingham Palace.

He then asked me to pass the salt, which I did.

I introduced myself, we ate our meals and he left the table telling me "Yes, I think we will be friends."

Kenneth was two people. He was the classically trained theatre actor with the dark brown voice projecting to the back row, or the cockney barrow-boy cum queen when he wanted to be smutty. He would be imparting some obscure Latin origin of a word, or grammatical inconsistency or he would be telling bawdy stories. One of his favourites was about bra shopping in Harrods with Maggie Smith who it seems when told the price of the bra she wished to buy had said, "Ow much? I'd rather ave me tits off"

Kenneth was a walk on the wild side for tea-time television. These things slipped through perhaps because no one actually realised what was being said.

Another thing which slipped through was when Richard received a tie, made for him by a fan that had the word COUNTDOWN appliqued down its length. Richard wore it held in place with a tie-pin positioned over the O, thanked the fan for their kind gift, and the programme went out in its entirety before anyone caught on to the problem.

Beverley disappeared after one series, and the other *vital statistician*, Linda, was unceremoniously dumped after the next leaving Carol Vorderman and me to continue. She looking like a librarian and I like a tart.

As time unfolded it became clear to me that YTV was run by highly efficient female PAs who propped up the male producers. These women ran the show from behind the scenes, putting papers before their bosses in the bar and getting signatures for things signed in a drunken haze. John Meade was a particularly extreme example of this, but he was not alone.

One night, at the end of a four-day run of filming, Carol and I went into the bar. After a short while Victoria Wood slipped in and stood alone quietly at the corner of the bar where she was soon joined by one of the producers who began talking to her in a menacing whisper. She looked as if she would die from embarrassment as his voice became louder and he threatened "If you ever disrupt my studio again like that, I will make sure you never work again in television."

She turned tail and left. She was wearing corduroy jodhpur style trousers with ankle boots, a shirt and a Fair-isle knitted waistcoat. A great look. However not one that her producer rated. She was not overtly sexual. Therefore, in his eyes she didn't count as a female. She had been reading a children's story and he had apparently been dismissive and disrespectful to her throughout that day's filming. She had risen above it with dignity. I have no idea what happened to him and I can't recall his name. Victoria Wood however wrote a scathing indictment of a Television studio later in her career which I recognised from beginning to end.

John Meade's presence hampered the production of our early series. Thankfully he focused on the guests in *Dictionary Corner* and was keen to influence their input as he believed they were there to inject the content. Carol and I were told "not to back ref" as it made the show harder to edit.

It was a great relief beginning a new block of programmes to be told that John had gone to Australia. We were given no allowance for clothes that season and had to re wear our previous outfits. Sandra, the PA told us his trip had used up the budget. She had put it through the system as *research*. Without his malevolent presence we all gelled and it was a joy to be there. We were regaled second hand with stories of how his ego was running wild over there. Jokes abounded of how on his first night he had been *rolled* whilst drunk at the Bar, and how he had explained that he had tried to explain that he had not been drunk but jet-lagged.

31

PICTURE THIS JOHN PLAYER SPECIALS

It's a Saturday afternoon in a bungalow in Knaresborough. Jack is laid on the sofa. Dot is pottering in the garden.

Jack calls out. "I'll have me block of Cadbury's Dairy Milk now, Dot."

She is in the lounge like a greyhound out of its trap. She has been anticipating this moment. "No, you won't, because there isn't any," she says confrontationally.

"Why is that?" Jack, alerted by the rebellion in the air, asks tentatively. "There is none, because the housekeeping won't stretch to it. That's why," says Dot triumphantly.

Jack leaps up from the sofa, goes into his bedroom opens the top cupboard of his wardrobe and takes out a black shiny cylindrical tub on which the gold writing reads *John Player Special*. He comes back into the lounge where Dot stands, hands on hips.

"What's this?" she demands.

"I'll tell you what this is. This is a tub of your cigarettes. The cigarettes that we said we had given up when they went up in the last budget. That's what this is."

Dots hands fall from her hips.

Jack continues. "Each one of the cigarettes represents a packet of 20 that I have found in your handbag. You work it out how much money there is here that has gone up in smoke in your sneaky little garden shed."

Dot is searching for something to say. Then it comes to her. " YOU said we were giving up. I didn't. I never said I would give up and how dare you go in my handbag!"

"Well. What can't speak can't lie," says Jack, delivering his coup-de-grace. "That's why I can't have my Cadbury's Dairy Milk. That's where all the bloody housekeeping is going."

"You shitehawk," cries Dot and flees the room.

Jack paces the lounge and Dot takes a bottle of vodka and twenty John Player Specials to her shed and pours herself a stiff one. Emboldened by three quarters of the bottle, Dot stumbles into the lounge and hits Jack across his head from behind. He jumps to his feet and punches her in the eye. Crying hysterically Dot throws a few random articles of clothes into her hold-all, gets on her scooter and unbelievably navigates her wobbly way successfully to Lincolnshire.

She arrives there just as her third daughter Helen, and family are loading up their car to go away on a boating trip on the Norfolk Broads. She pours out her incoherent tale and Helen dispenses tea and sympathy before bowing to pressure from the family wanting to be off and shows Dot to a spare bedroom advising her to "Sleep it off."

Dot does sleep it off and busies herself whilst the family are away. When they come back she has purchased a caravan and installed it in a corner of their garden. She has part exchanged her scooter for a *Datsun Cherry*. She has been to see a solicitor and has had the bank account frozen. She is here for the long haul. Helen is backed into a corner. Not unlike the caravan!

32

ROOM 101

John Meade returns from Australia. Cast and crew are like children returned to school in September after their summer break. John senses rebellion in the air as he forces us to perform various lame pilot programmes which his *research* in Australia has provided. These he believes will be the winners that will be great *spin offs* from *Countdown*. Among the imposed changes is Kenneth's replacement by Giles Brandreth. I am sad, as Kenneth and I had become close.

On one occasion a fan letter had got through to me un-read by the usual filtering process. In the letter a woman told me that I sucked, my clothes were crumpled, and my hair was a mess. I took it into the next dressing room and showed it to Kenneth.

"Ah, the fucking green ink brigade. Take no notice." He screwed it into a ball and threw it into the waste paper bin. "Whatever you do half of them will love you and half of them will hate you. That's where that belongs. This show is full of weird and singularly unattractive people. Can you imagine the mentality of this person to put pen to paper to say all this ?"

I smiled gratefully but knew there was in fact some truth in it. John was bored and so always trying to break the record of how many programmes we could make in a day. The record was eight. By the end of a week of that regime, running from the studio, changing outfits and running back to go again we were exhausted and it did not make for magnificence.

During the time Kenneth and I spent together he told me how the *Carry On* Films had ruined his career and that was why he was reduced to doing shit like this. He could have been a serious classical actor. Now he had to put up with proles shouting "Ooo Matron" at him when he was trying to buy his intimate toiletries in Boots the Chemist. He was annoyed if people recognised him. He was beside himself it they didn't. He would go through intricate charades to be noticed. He told me how he never had sex because he was a blood donor and took that very seriously. He spoke with great reverence about Joe, but as yet my education did not run to knowing to whom he referred and there was no Google in those days.

Giles was incredible. He was a godsend for the programme. He could *fill* for hours and was enthusiastic and refreshing. We jogged along for hundreds of programmes over the years, John getting more and more out of control. He would sidle up to me when the studio audience was in, and I was miked up and whisper, "When I were in t'bath this mornin avin' a wank I were thinkin' of you."

Another time. "Don't wear the fuckin 'orrible jumper again, you looked like a rugby stuff bag. All people want from you is tits an teeth."

Carol once made a suggestion for improving the format of the show and was rewarded with "You do t'fuckin sums and I'll produce t'fuckin programme."

Rumours were rife about who was going to get the chop. The sword of Damocles even hung over Richard for a good while.

One day the studio broke for lunch an hour early. Thinking nothing about it I went to the dressing room to change into something comfortable.

Glancing up at the monitor I saw the current Miss YTV, a seventeen-year-old, standing by the letters board and being counted in by the floor manager. The monitors in reception, make-up, Wardrobe, and elsewhere were all broadcasting this sight around the building. I was drawing sympathetic comments from shocked people in all the departments. I went to the dressing room and began to pack up my things ready to leave when Carol said, "Don't you dare give in. You have as much right to be here as him. Don't give him the pleasure."

We stayed in the dressing room and I must admit I made a special effort with my appearance for when we went back in to the studio that afternoon.

As I walked away from the warm up man and the Studio Audience John cheerily said, "...and by the way, that wasn't a fuckin' audition for your fuckin' job, I just promised her a fuckin' screen test."

"Oh really," I replied. " Was she no good, John?"

That afternoon was the end of our block of committed dates and Carol and I went into the bar as usual. We were seated at a table with some of the crew when John walked in. He was sandwiched between Miss YTV and her mate, both of whom were much taller than he was, with an arm across the shoulder of each of them.

"Look at him," I said. "He's like a dog with two dicks."

"No, he's not," said Carol. "He's a dick with two dogs."

During this period of time my parents were separated and my mother was pushing for a divorce. She was resident at my sister's home in Lincoln in an increasingly fraught situation. Jack was on his own in the bungalow in Knaresborough. I would take food from the hospitality buffet over to him on evenings when we finished filming in time and listen to his self-pitying re-telling of the situation and all its injustices. He had thrown out all the cups that had chips in them. He had made a key-rack and labelled all the keys to every part of the house. He had tidied out that drawer that everyone has in their kitchens that contains all the vital stuff you never knew you had.

When I stupidly mentioned to him the humiliating Miss YTV audition, Jacks considered opinion was, "Well our Cath, you've only been cashing in on the good looks and physique I gave you up to now. You will soon find out. No-one wants a fairy when they are forty."

Time passed and the best I could hope for from John Meade was to be ignored. His mother came into studio once with him and she was uncannily like Jack's mother. Hinge and Bracket in appearance and *sloppy stern*, as Larkin would have put it, in attitude. I saw John Meade reduced to a little boy in her presence in exactly the same way.

In around nineteen-eighty-four we were all assembled in *The Queens Hotel* for a social gathering. There was much back-patting and ego-stroking going on. I was amazed when, making one of his self-congratulatory speeches, John Meade referred to me in a jocular way as "The future Mrs. Meade." This was some change of attitude and I was immediately suspicious. Rightly so, as when I went up to my room and got into bed, John Meade was in it. I handled it as diplomatically as I could and eventually bundled him and his clothes out of the room. The dye was cast. This was the end.

At the end of the next series I received the anticipated call from the booking department and was told that my contract would not be renewed.

The last series was tense. John never made eye contact with me and everyone knew what was going on. My clothing allowance was zero and I bought my own clothes. On the last programme at the very end Richard signed off saying that they would be back soon for the next series all except me "...who was off, just for a short while to do something else, with Michael Parkinson.". It was true I was booked to do some *Give Us A Clue* but the rest was calculated to cause the least attention possible.

My mike was faded down so I smiled weakly and accepted the bouquet of flowers waving a cheery goodbye.

There were farewell drinks in the bar during the lunch break, where my replacement Karen, whom I had worked with, took my place. They went back into studio to begin recording the next series and I left.

She feels as if she's in a play as The Beatles line goes. Looking back, I have always handled stress and fear in the same way. I slipped into some kind of alternate reality and was watching myself. I drove back along the M62 in the pouring rain, crying and playing melancholy music. I arranged for my daughter to go to stay with my sister-in-law overnight and drank and smoked whilst listening to Peter Gabriel and Kate Bush. *Don't give up, you've still got friends.* It was painful and melodramatic.

The next morning I woke up feeling fine for a few seconds, as one does, until I remembered the situation. Last night had shocked me. It was frightening. I carried on with normal life and, as my feelings settled, I realised that things had to change. Jack's words, "No-one wants a fairy when they are forty," were in my head. I knew he was racist, violent, undermining, bitter and misogynistic and that he was best ignored. However, this time he had a point. He was right if by accident. I had allowed myself to be treated this way. In mitigation the times were like that, but this was not a safe world to be in.

Over the next week or so my thoughts cleared and I made a decision. No more of this…I would apply to go to University, retrain and do something useful.

33
LAST REFUSAL

A couple of months later I had embarked upon a course in Literary studies at Manchester university.

I had been so apprehensive the first time I was due to go to class, that I went and got pissed instead. It was like Hilda Baker reads the classics.

"Who? Never heard of them. What? I didn't know that. When? Well I never!"

I asked to borrow someone's copy of Homer's *Iliac*. That's how much I had to learn.

Then one day the phone went and it was Sandra from Yorkshire TV. John hated my replacement. Would I consider coming back? My reply came out of my mouth completely bypassing my brain. As I said what I said it was as much news to me as it must have been to Sandra. "That's most kind of you. If I am ever masochistic enough to want more of that treatment I will bear your offer in mind.“

Shocked Sandra replied, "But it would be more money and there would be spin-off programmes. Your career would really take off."

"No thanks, Sandra. I can see where all this is leading. Trying to cling on to the wreckage. Trying to keep my profile up by doing shitty reality programmes. More plastic surgery as I age and try to look young. Pantomime at Christmas. Wheeled out for advertisements of dodgy moral content. I think I will pass, my love."

"Ok," said Sandra. "Always remember you were asked.“

"I will, but I will take my chances in obscurity, thanks all the same." And that is where we left it.

34
EPILOGUE

Now we have got to the end. I thank you and hope it wasn't a bore. I wrote this during lockdown in the time of Corona virus 2020. I am now seventy and have had to self-isolate. I realise that for a portion of the population this has been a time of great suffering. For me it has been a time to take stock, slow down, take pleasure in creative things and be still.

I conclude that there is no way the world can stay locked down and sooner or later this virus will run its course. That's what they do. They cull the herd until there is herd immunity. That surely is what everyone is not saying.

There is no reality other than the reality created by those in charge at any given time. Whether you were a citizen of ancient Rome who went off to the communal toilets every morning or a little old lady in Peru chewing on coca leaves, or even if you live here where we invite Siri or Cortana into our homes with their ever open microphones in order that we can ask them to play us a tune or to turn out the lights, it feels like reality to us.

Part of our communal delusion is that there will always be a happy ending. That is not so. There could be a meteor strike, we could be invaded by aliens and vaporised, the whole galaxy could be swallowed into a black hole, monkeys could suddenly mutate and take charge, venting thousands of years of resentment. I don't know. Neither do you. However, the chances of our being here are so infinitesimally remote, and clever as we are, we have no idea what is really going on so I have decided the best I can do is hope that I am part of some giant cosmic constant re-defining of atoms. Our time on this earth is short. There is not another go.

I remember in a Kurt Vonnegut novel there are aliens called Tralfamadorians who have many more senses than we do and so see a human being as a centipede type creature that is a baby at one end and an old person at the other. "The best thing to do is to collect string" as Woody Allen had one of his characters, Zellig, say. No, the best thing to do is to be still, calm, decent, and take pleasure in nature, oh yes and ' avoid those who are vexatious to the spirit.

It is my hope that we come out of the Corona situation with our values changed. I hope that we carry on the things that make the world less ravaged. I hope we continue to value those who do worthwhile jobs. I hope all our appreciation of them during these times continues, and that we were not just *blowing smoke up their asses* because we needed them. I hope we don't go back to worshipping false idols. Oh yes, and whilst I am hoping, would it be too much to ask that President Trump caught a really bad dose of this virus?

If we end up in lockdown number two I shall write part two of this little epistle. If I am part of the cull, you will never know about the second part of my life. Hey Ho!

I have purposely not included my daughter in this as hers is not my story to tell. All I will say is that I love her most in the world but wish I had been better at it.

I have spared you, Dear Reader, the highs and lows of my relationships with men. Otherwise we would have been here until the cows come home. To enlist the pay-off line of a well-known legal joke, I am 'better informed, but no wiser!' Even after all that research.

I leave you for no reason whatsoever, with a snapshot of life that my daughter and I witnessed together and recorded in our different ways.

35
I LICK YOUR FANNY EXISTENTIALLY

Sitting in our Vauxhall Nova,
Just outside his council flat,
when they sprang from round the corner.
"We're three dogs, and that is that."

He was big and black and Bear-like,
One was sort of terriery,
She was little, a *Jane Russell*.
In this setting, so Mike Leigh.

Just what bonds these three together?
Just what keeps their friendship strong?
In this tussocky savannah,
Just what makes them pal along?

Or is it that they're thrown together,
These three mutts from Fallowfield?
Were these three just born for pleasure?
Born so free, so here, so wild.

As they trotted down the entry,
No pre-amble. No fore-play,
His 'long tong' just licked her fanny
"Once for luck", as one might say.

No, "May I?", "Shall we?", "Would you care to?"
Just, "Cop for that, you temptress, you."
Just "Fait accompli", same old one two,
A DOG DOES, WHAT A DOG CAN DO..

NB. in Manchester they often say 'tong' not 'tongue'

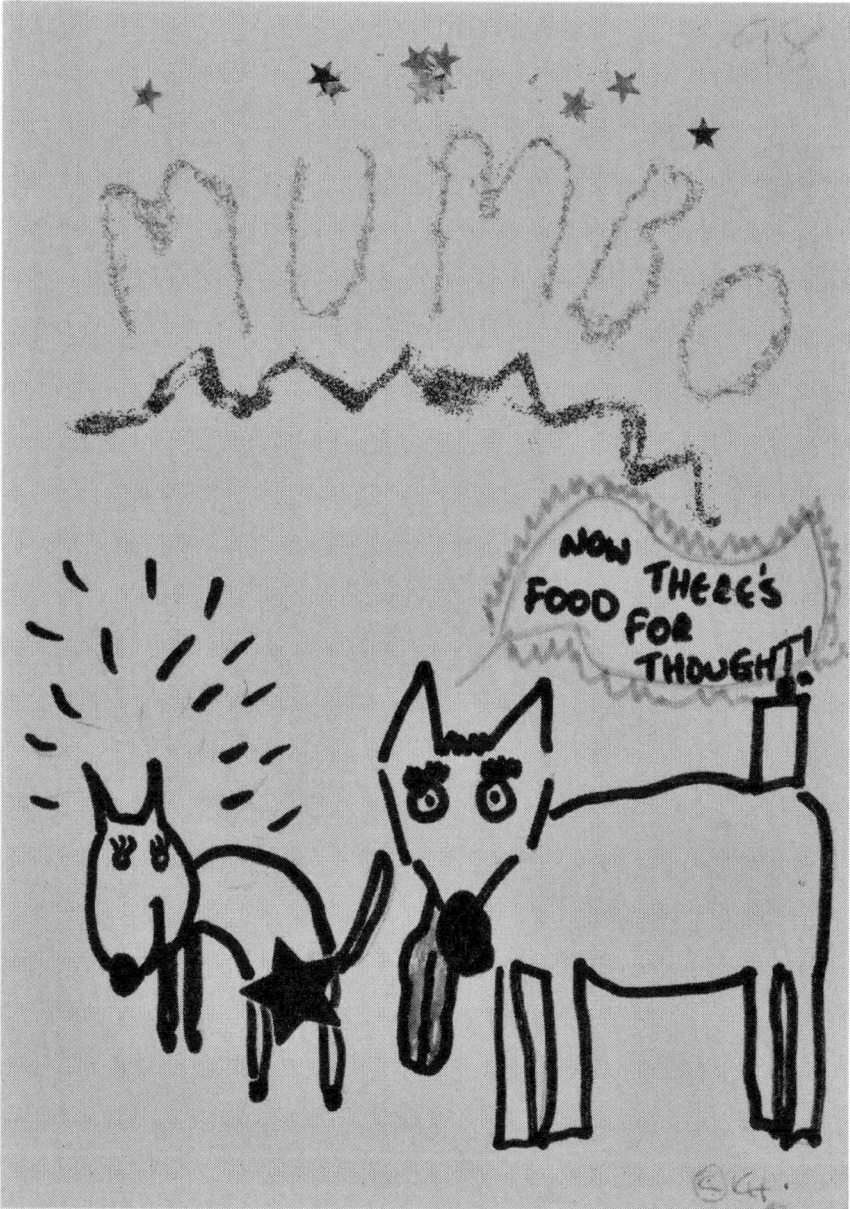

ACKNOWLEDGMENTS

Writing this has been cathartic. I wish to thank the following people:

Elaine who said to me "Ere Caffrin, why dontcha write yer buk during this lockdarn" and who read every page as we went along telling me that she loved it.

Val, who proof read my manuscript and indeed is the "Val" who kept Pen and I alive with the tins of M&S food during our Withington years.

Lee, ever generous, who shared his contact with me for getting my manuscript read and published, a thing, it would seem, that people are often reluctant to do.

And of course to Andrew for believing in me, reading, editing and publishing this book.

APS PUBLICATIONS

Printed in Great Britain
by Amazon